A PRIMER FOR CHRISTIAN DOCTRINE

A Primer for Christian Doctrine

Jonathan R. Wilson

WILLIAM B. EERDMANS PUBLISHING COMPANY
GRAND RAPIDS, MICHIGAN / CAMBRIDGE, U.K.

Wm. B. Eerdmans Publishing Co.
255 Jefferson Ave. S.E., Grand Rapids, Michigan 49503 /
P.O. Box 163, Cambridge CB3 9PU U.K.

Printed in the United States of America

10 09 08 07 06 05   7 6 5 4 3 2 1

Library of Congress Cataloging-in-Publication Data

Wilson, Jonathan R.
A primer for Christian doctrine / Jonathan R. Wilson.
p.   cm.
ISBN 0-8028-4656-4 (pbk.)
1. Theology, Doctrinal.   I. Title.

BT75.3.W55   2005
230 — dc22

2005040499

www.eerdmans.com

In memory of

Thomas A. Langford, Jr.
(1929-2000)

Contents

CONTENTS

Contents

Acknowledgments

My greatest debt is to my students. During my years on the faculty at Westmont College (1989-2003), I taught over 2,000 first year students in a required course on Christian doctrine. These lively and challenging students forced me to be clear and careful in my teaching. To the extent that I have achieved clarity and care in this book, it is the result of the training I received during those years. I am grateful to the students, faculty, and administration of Westmont for their formative work in my life and teaching.

Since joining the faculty of Acadia Divinity College in July 2003, I have been aided by teaching assistants and students who have read and commented on the text. Scott Kohler and Thelma McLeod deserve special thanks for their careful reading. Michael Swalm has helped with the preparation of the index.

My wife, Marti, has this year participated in my course on theology and read this manuscript. It is a joy to be her partner, to teach her and be taught by her in our common calling to delight in God and follow Jesus Christ.

This book is dedicated to Tom Langford, my last formal teacher of theology, who shaped and inspired me with his intellectual discipline, spiritual passion, and deep conviction that "theology is for life." I am grateful.

Preface

This book is neither a highly condensed systematic theology nor a very short summary of Christian doctrine. It is a primer — a first book of Christian doctrine intended to help you understand what Christians mean when we talk about "doctrine" and "theology."

I have written this book for new students of theology and doctrine. My aim is to tell you what your teachers hope you already know when you begin your formal study of doctrine. Some years ago you would not have needed a book like this. Back then (the "good old days"?), what I am going to tell you in this book would have been topics for discussion around the dinner table, in church parking lots, in kitchens and on fishing boats. Today, the church seems generally to be less interested in "doctrine."

Perhaps there's a good side to this. We are not as divided or condemning as we once were. Today, some of the issues that used to divide Christians seem unimportant. At the same time, however, the beliefs that we hold are an essential part of who we are as Christians. So the trick is to set aside the trivial differences while also holding firmly to the beliefs that identify us. As we do so, we may appreciate the differences among Christians while also avoiding the conclusion that what people believe does not matter. There is a big difference between saying, "We can't know some things," and saying, "We can't know anything." There's also a big difference between saying, "We can't be certain about everything," and saying, "We can't be certain about anything." This book is first an introduction to what we Christians know with certainty about God and God's work of creation and redemption.

In this book I will guide you through your first study of Christian doctrine. If you were planning a visit to an unfamiliar city, you might purchase a guidebook for that city. Now, you can certainly visit a new city without having a guidebook. And you can learn a lot about a city without visiting it, just by reading a guidebook. But the best practice is to visit the city with the best guidebook you can find.

This "guidebook" for Christian doctrine is no different. You can study systematic theology or Christian doctrine without this guide. And you can read this guide without at the same time studying Christian doctrine. But the best practice is to read this book as a guide to a "big book" in doctrine or theology.

This book is different from a city guidebook in two important ways. First, unlike a guidebook, which may be for only one city, this book is not a guide to only one theology, whether written by a particular theologian or from a particular church tradition, such as Baptist or Methodist or Pentecostal or Roman Catholic. Instead, I have tried to write this book so that it can guide you through almost any study of Christian doctrine. Secondly, unlike a city guidebook, which is usually directed toward tourists who will eventually return to their homes, this book is directed toward disciples who will make their study of theology the basis for a lifetime of learning to follow Jesus Christ.

Preliminary Definitions of Theology and Doctrine

In the previous paragraph I used terms like "theology" and "Christian doctrine" to describe what I am guiding you through. These terms identify a particular way of studying and explaining Christianity. The approach to Christianity that I am orienting you to in this book seeks to identify, describe, and commend beliefs that Christians have about God, the world (including human beings), and the relationship between them. Since this is a guide to *Christ*ian doctrine, what Christians believe about Jesus Christ will be central. Other beliefs about God and the world will have a strong connection to what Christians believe about Jesus Christ.

Christian doctrine is not the only way to study, explain, and commend Christianity. We may also study the Bible and the history of the church. The best way to learn the differences among these approaches is simply to study them, but I will try to give some explanation of their differences here. Since the Christian Bible — the Old and New Testaments — tells us about Jesus Christ, Christians place great emphasis on studying the Bible. This study may be concerned with its history, its cultures, its languages, and its teaching about God, Jesus, and the world. Since "theology" is concerned with the last things on that list, there is a lot of overlap between the study of Christian doctrine and the study of the Bible. The difference is that "theology," as I mean it here, seeks to summarize the teaching of the Bible, learn from the ways Christians have understood it through history, and think about our present lives as Christians. So, for example, where biblical study might focus on what Paul, one of the authors in the New Testament, teaches about the death of Christ, theology will try to summarize and systematize the whole of what the Bible says about the death of Christ. So, Christian doctrine will try to give an account of the meaning of the death of Christ that considers what all of the Old and New Testament teaches about Christ. But that's not all theology does.

The study of Christian doctrine also learns from the history of the church. Throughout the ages, faithful Christians have written and studied Christian doctrine. Their attempts to explain and commend what Christians believe are examples of how to think about God and the world, and the relationship between them. So, in the study of Christian doctrine we will often ask, "What did the church teach about Christian doctrine in previous centuries?" Our attempts to answer this question are meant to help us learn from faithful followers of Jesus Christ in previous times and places so that we can be faithful today.

Finally, then, Christian doctrine seeks to help us be faithful to Jesus Christ today. As new generations are born, we must continually present the claims of Christianity so that others may become followers of Jesus Christ. Moreover, we continually face new challenges to Christian faith. Some of these come from within the church. We must always be on guard against drifting away from Christian doctrine, so we must practice a "critical" theology that seeks to correct our tendency to drift off course. Other challenges come from outside the church. Society and culture are continually changing, so we must continually seek to describe what it means to be a faithful Christian *today*.

Design of This Book

In this book I will help you understand Christian doctrine by explaining why Christian theology covers particular topics. I will also explain which subjects are treated under various topics and why some theologians start in different places or leave out certain topics or treat them in a different order. That means that the full effectiveness of this book depends largely on your own study of theology, formally in a classroom or informally through your own reading.

The book is designed so that you may read the chapters in any order. If the theology you are studying approaches Christian doctrine in an order that differs from this guide, that's okay. Read the chapters in this book in the order used by the theology you are studying. If your other text has chapters or topics that do not correspond to this book's chapter titles, look for the topics in the subsections of the chapters in my table of contents. If that fails, then check out the index. If you don't find your topic at all, you may still discover it in one of my chapters, or you may discover that the theology you are studying is unusual in its treatment of the topic.

The first chapter of this book discusses some of the preliminary issues that most theologians consider as they organize their theology. Where do we start? Why start there? What order do we give to various doctrines? What is the purpose of theology? The following chapters then discuss various topics that usually occur in some way in Christian theology. Each of these chapters describes what may be covered under that topic, why those issues fit under that particular topic, how various theologians approach those issues, why they assign different degrees of importance to them, and why they may leave out some issues.

You will need to find out whether it works better for you to read this book before or after you read your theological text. Of course, you may want to read this book all the way through before starting the other study. However, if you do, you will probably be helped if you return to this book as you continue your study of Christian doctrine.

I can think of no greater privilege than having the time, freedom, and ability to study theology. It is a source of constant joy for me. I hope that you find it to be the same for you. And I hope that this book may make a small contribution to that enjoyment.

CHAPTER 1

Introduction

As you begin your study of Christian doctrine, it would be helpful for you to know what Christian doctrine is all about. How is Christian doctrine different from studying the Bible? How is doctrine related to practical issues of the Christian life? What is the relationship between doctrine and the history of the church? What is the relationship between Christian doctrine and other disciplines like philosophy, sociology, or physics?

The best way to learn what Christian doctrine is, is to study it. As you study it, you will find that your understanding will deepen and your answers to the questions above will develop. Sometimes you will learn to ask better questions and new questions. Growing intellectually and spiritually is not always a matter of finding answers; sometimes it is a matter of learning what the important questions are.

Even though you will learn more about Christian doctrine by studying it, it is important to at least have some orientation to it as you begin. The simplest way to understand doctrine is to think of it as "teachings." So, Christian "doctrine" studies the teachings of Christianity. These teachings are rooted in the Bible and have been developed by the church over the centuries. Some doctrines have been believed and taught by most Christians, in most places and times. Others have generated significant disagreements among Christians. One of the tasks of learning doctrine is to learn to distinguish the essentials from the nonessentials. And of course, not all Christians agree on what is essential and what is nonessential.

Why Study Doctrine?

If Christians have not always agreed on doctrine, then you may ask, "Why study doctrine?" Wouldn't it be better just to ignore doctrine and get on with the practical issues of the Christian life? This kind of question and the attempt to avoid doctrine ignores several important factors.

First, there is simply no way to separate the Christian life from what we believe. How we live is connected to what we believe. Sometimes this connection is clear and well thought out. At other times it is unclear and not thought out. At still other times, how we live contradicts what we claim to believe. The study of doctrine helps Christians check the connection between how we live and what we believe. That process can be painful when we discover that we are not really living out what we say we believe. At other times the process can be delightful, when we discover the reasons for why we live the way we do. This is the process of growing up in the faith.

Secondly, to be a Christian is to be a theologian. Even if you are not a Christian, to study Christianity or to consider it means that you must for a time be a theologian. Theology is basically the study of Christian doctrine. (There are more distinctions to theology that I will introduce later.) If you think about God at all, you are doing theology, because theology is the study of God (from the Greek *Theos,* "God"). So the question is not whether you are a theologian or not. Rather, the question is whether you are going to be careful and informed, or careless and ignorant, in your thinking about God.

Thirdly, the study of doctrine helps Christians pass the gospel on faithfully and accurately to the next generation of believers. The study of doctrine also helps us present the good news of

Jesus Christ clearly and faithfully to those who do not believe. The mission of the church is to proclaim the gospel — the good news of Jesus Christ. We can do this only if we have thought clearly and carefully about that gospel.

Jesus Christ himself exemplifies this concern for doctrine, for right thinking about God. He was constantly challenging and correcting people's ideas about God. Many of his public encounters with the scribes and Pharisees were intellectual contests. Who would win the allegiance and the faith of the people who were listening? Would it be Jesus or someone else? Likewise, Jesus' times with his followers were often times of instruction in the truth about God. Paul also calls Christians to guard the gospel and to think carefully about God. Over the centuries Christians have followed Jesus' example and heeded Paul's call. The result is Christian doctrine.

Why study Christian doctrine? Because we want to connect what we believe with how we live. Because we can't avoid Christian doctrine if we are going to consider the claims of Christianity. Because we who are Christians are called to careful thinking by the mission we have been given, by the example of Jesus, Paul, and the church.

Theology and Doctrine

Earlier I introduced the word "theology." Because theology is the study of God, it is possible to have theology that isn't Christian. That is, it is possible to study the doctrines of other religions. So, for example, we could study Jewish theology. One complication may be found in the argument that theology is primarily a Christian development and that when we apply it to other religions, we are imposing on them a Christian notion. That argument need not concern us here, because we will be concerned in this book simply with Christian theology and Christian doctrine.

Even when we restrict theology to Christianity, there are still some significant distinctions. Because theology broadly means

3

the study of doctrine or teachings, we can talk about the "theology of Paul," "New Testament theology," "Old Testament theology," and "biblical theology." If we study the history of Christian doctrines, we call that "historical theology." Some will speak also of "practical theology" when they study the application of Christian doctrine to practices of the church, such as Christian living or pastoral theology. The applications of the term "theology" are almost endless.

In this book we are concerned with theology and Christian doctrine as the systematic study and presentation of Christian teachings. That study involves the teaching of the Bible, the history of doctrines, and even how we practice our faith. So as we study Christian doctrine, we will not be setting aside these other theologies (Paul, NT, historical, etc.). Instead, we will be incorporating them into our purpose as it develops.

To this point I have been referring to theology as the study of God. Now it is time to broaden the term a bit, because we Christians believe that Christianity is not only about God, it is also about humankind. And if God is the creator and redeemer of the universe, then theology is ultimately about everything. That is obviously a project that we will never complete. Nevertheless, we are called by God to begin that task with faith in God's provision, with humility about our own abilities, and in community with other Christians.

Doctrines and Disagreements

As you approach the study of Christian doctrine, you probably have an implicit, unexamined theology that you have absorbed from Christians you have known — your church, your family, your friends. One of the disorienting experiences of studying doctrine more carefully and explicitly is discovering that Christians do not all believe exactly the same way. Of course, you know this deep down, but studying doctrine brings it to the surface and makes you face it. Moreover, studying theology will increase the number of questions you have. Some of your questions will be answered, but new, more difficult ones may arise.

Actually, we should expect these disagreements and difficulties. After all, theology is the study of God and the world. If we can't understand ourselves or the world fully, how can we expect to understand God fully? Of course there are going to be disagreements. At the same time, because we Christians believe that God has revealed Godself to us, we can approach the study of God with confidence. At the conclusion of this part of your study, you will know more about differences among Christians, but you will also know more about agreements among Christians. One of the aims of Christian doctrine is that your understanding of God and the world will be richer. That will happen as you learn how other Christians view God and the world.

The Method of Theology

"Method" can mean a lot of things. Here I simply mean how we do theology. Some theologians think that the best way to learn the method of theology is simply to do it, so they provide very little if any introduction to how to do theology. This doesn't mean they don't have a method, it simply means they don't want to see the method as something that can be separated from actually doing theology. Other theologians think it is important for you to have some grasp of method before you begin to do theology, otherwise you may feel lost and never really figure out what is going on. To help you understand the issues of method in theology, we will consider three topics: structure, sources, and authority.

Although theology concerns itself with everything, a presentation of Christian doctrine has to begin somewhere and display some sort of coherent pattern. That is the question of structure. Theologians must also make decisions about the sources for their theology. To what extent will they draw on the Bible, church history, experience, social conditions, and other disciplines such as philosophy? That is the question of sources. At the same time, theologians must also decide how much weight to give the various elements of theology. Will they weigh their various sources equally, or will one have greater weight? If two sources are in conflict, which one rules over the other? That is the question of authority.

These three — structure, sources, and authority — are intertwined. Where a person begins her presentation of doctrine may not reflect the final authority. For example, to make a connection with students a teacher may begin with experience, but the authority that guides her account of doctrine may be the Bible. Some theologians make their decisions about these issues very clear and explicit, usually at the beginning of their work. Others incorporate these decisions into their presentations so that you learn them as you learn doctrine.

One of your first goals as you study doctrine should be to discern the structure, sources, and authority of the theology you are studying. You may revise your judgment later, but it is always helpful to begin with some provisional understanding. To help you accomplish that goal, we will consider each of these in more detail.

Structure

There is no set pattern for the presentation of Christian doctrine. If you study several theologians, you may discover some similarities in pattern. Although theologians choose different starting points and structures, in the end most cover the same doctrines, even though they do so in different ways.

The starting point for teaching doctrine varies among theologians. Some start with experience and build an understanding of doctrine that reflects on our experience. Their presentation may clarify, correct, and expand the experience with which they started. Others start with the Bible, developing its teaching in a systematic way and making connections with our lives. Still others start with the history of theology and the teaching of the church, then move to the Bible and experience. Today, some theologians begin their study of doctrine with social conditions, such as injustice and poverty, and then explore how Christianity responds to those conditions.

Theologians also make decisions about how to present Christian doctrine. What order should the presentation take? Where should various doctrines be located? Most theologians begin with an introduction to their theology, where they make explicit some of the decisions that we are considering. Sometimes this presentation is very brief, often because the theologian wants you to learn about method in the midst of doing theology. Other theologians provide an extensive introduction, because they want you to understand the method before you begin to do theology.

Sources

As theologians make decisions about structure, they are also making decisions about "sources." I am using the term broadly here to include not only the sources of guidance and insight a theologian might use, but also sources of challenge or opposition to Christian doctrine. Often decisions about the use of sources are tied to decisions about authority, but the relationship is not always straightforward, as we will see below when we consider authority in Christian doctrine. The way a theologian uses sources is typically tied to judgments about the authority of the source.

Roughly speaking (there are almost always exceptions to any general statement about theologians), the more "conservative" theologians are, the more they will use the Bible as a source. For some theologians, Christian doctrine is primarily the systematic presentation of the teaching found throughout the Bible. So, for example, a theologian might gather the teaching on creation from Genesis, the Psalms, Isaiah, the letters of Paul and Peter, as well as other biblical passages, and systematize these teachings and present them in contemporary thought forms. Other theologians use the Bible more indirectly, treating it as the source of a vision of God and the world. The theologian then develops this vision as an account of Christian doctrine. Still other theologians may use the Bible only occasionally as a source, judging it to be the product of earlier ages where people believed things about the world that we no longer believe.

Roughly speaking (again), the more "liberal" theologians are, the more they will use experience as a source. For such theologians, Christian doctrine is the development of symbols that represent our experience as people of faith. The teaching we find in Scripture gives us the symbols that previous generations found useful for representing their experience. Today, we may find other symbols more effective. So, for example, in the Bible we may find sin captured by the idea of breaking God's law. Today, however, such an idea, such a symbol, does not effectively express our experience. Thus, the task of theology is to find a new symbol that effectively expresses our experience.

Some theologians will place great weight on the history of doctrine or tradition as a source for theology. Over the centuries the church has developed statements of doctrine called creeds, confessions, and catechisms. "Creed" usually refers to a statement developed by the church before the various splits in the church. "Confession" typically refers to a statement produced by one particular tradition. A catechism is a statement developed by a particular tradition for use in teaching the full scope of doctrine believed by that tradition. It is used primarily to prepare believers for baptism, confirmation, and church membership. For some church traditions, these statements are essential to the work of theology. Most Christians accept the earliest creeds of the church, such as the Apostles' Creed and the Nicene Creed. Other traditions look to confessions and catechisms that were developed within their own history. For example, some of the churches that trace their heritage back to John Calvin, the Protestant Reformer of the sixteenth century, may look to the Heidelberg Catechism or the Westminster Confession and Catechism. Recently, the Catholic Church has produced a new catechism for its members.

Not all theologians make use of the history of Christian doctrine in their theology. Just as some theologians regard the Bible as a product of previous ages where the world was viewed differently than it is viewed today, so also some theologians regard creeds, confessions, and catechisms as "time-bound" and "culture-bound" statements that are of little if any use to us today in a new time and culture.

In recent decades an increasing number of theologians have turned as a source for theology to social conditions, including poverty, injustice, oppression, and marginalization. Drawing on biblical texts such as Exodus (God frees the enslaved Israelites), the OT prophets (who condemn the oppression of widows, orphans, and the poor), and Jesus' ministry to the poor and outcast, these theologians make race, class, and gender important categories for theology. Most of them can be loosely grouped together as liberation theologians because their theology emphasizes the socially liberating power of the gospel.

Finally, we should note that some theologians draw significantly on other disciplines. Traditionally, theology and philosophy have been in close conversation with each other. Their subject matter and their history overlap considerably. Sociology, psychology, literature, and the natural sciences may also be addressed at various points in an account of Christian doctrine.

Authority

At the same time that theologians are weaving together various sources for their accounts of Christian doctrine, they are also making judgments about the relative authority of those sources. Usually, they make these judgments clear, either in an explicit statement or by the way they use various sources.

I have already noted how some theologians set aside the Bible and the history of doctrine as authoritative guides for us today. But to see how the use of sources as authoritative can be complex, we will consider different ways of using experience in the work of theology. For many theologians, experience is an important element in Christian doctrine. What if we arrive at a point in our study of doctrine where there seems to be a conflict between our understanding of our experience and our interpretation of the Bible? At this point some theologians will grant authority to experience and adjust their interpretation of the Bible to fit our interpretation of our experience. Some will say that the Bible, not just our interpretation of the Bible, is wrong. Other theologians will grant authority to our interpretation of the Bible and adjust their interpretation of experience to conform to the Bible.

Doctrine and the Bible

Because the Bible is such an important part of Christian doctrine, we need to give it special attention. As I noted above, theologians vary in their judgments about the role and authority of the Bible. For some the Bible serves as a container of information. The task of Christian doctrine is to extract that information from the Bible and organize it into a coherent, logically consistent system. For others the Bible testifies to experiences that people of Christian faith have had. The task of Christian doctrine, then, is to find ways of conveying that same experience to people today. For still others, the Bible tells the story of God's work in the world. Here, the task of Christian doctrine is to guide the faithful presentation of that story so that others may enter into it today.

As theologians use the Bible in these various ways, they are also making judgments about its authority. However, these judgments do not always line up neatly with the various uses that are made of the Bible. For some theologians the Bible is inerrant. Some inerrantists hold that the Bible, interpreted correctly, is without error in all matters, including history, geography, science, and doctrine. Others hold that it is inerrant only on matters of faith and practice and may err on matters of geography, history, and science. Sometimes these latter theologians will describe the Bible as infallible rather than inerrant. But there is a subtle difference between inerrant and infallible. Inerrant refers properly to the content of the Bible: Does it teach the truth? Infallible refers to the purpose of the Bible: Does it accomplish its purpose? Other theologians may regard the Bible as authoritative without using terms like "inerrant" or "infallible."

There are also theologians that regard the Bible as an important source for theology but do not grant it any special authority. For them, as I noted above, the Bible is a product of previous cultures. Since the Enlightenment of the seventeenth and eighteenth centuries, human reason and science have changed the way we view the world. Thus, for these theologians the Bible stands as the founding document of Christianity, but we must correct it today by what we know from reason and science.

Behind these views of the authority of the Bible are judgments about God's involvement in the writing of Scripture. Those theologians who view the Bible as authoritative also tend to believe that God was directly involved in its writing. They use the term "inspiration" to identify the way God worked with the human authors of Scripture, though they vary in their accounts of inspiration. Those who do not regard the Bible as authoritative believe it is merely human accounts of experiences, unaided by God. Thus, when they correct or set aside the teaching of the Bible, they are only doing what we do with any other piece of literature, though they acknowledge that the Bible has special status for Christians as our "founding document."

Theological Style

As you study Christian doctrine, you will quickly learn that theologians have different theological styles. By this I do not mean writing styles exactly. Rather, I mean that some theologians are more scientific and others are more artistic. Theologians who practice a "scientific style" are rigorous in their argumentation.

They carefully qualify their statements; they make logical connections in their presentations and give reasons for their conclusions. We may say they write for our ears and make their appeal to our minds. Theologians who practice an "artistic style" are painting a picture. They use colorful language; they make imaginative connections and draw us into their vision. We may say they write for our eyes and make their appeal to our hearts. Of course, a few theologians do both; for them we should be especially thankful.

Ultimately, Christian doctrine should address our ears and our eyes, appeal to our minds and our hearts. The purpose of Christian doctrine is not merely to make us more knowledgeable but to make us more mature as followers of Jesus Christ, to make us more like him. My hope and prayer is that this book will aid you in that process.

CHAPTER 2

God

Of course Christians believe in God. All the creeds of the church begin with that confession: "I believe in God . . ." But others also believe in God — Jews, Moslems, philosophical theists (who believe in God but do not connect that belief to religious faith), and many more. When a Christian says, "I believe in God," is the Christian saying the same thing a Jew or Moslem is saying by using those same words?

Christian theologians may sometimes argue about an answer to this question. But if we turn to the Bible or the creeds, the answer is clear: Christians mean something very particular when we confess belief in God. In the Old Testament, the God in whom Christians believe chooses one people, Israel. In the New Testament, the God in whom we believe comes to us in Jesus Christ.

As the early church reflected on this history of God's revelation, they summarized it in various creeds. These creeds help guide our understanding of God's revelation. None of them says simply, "I believe in God." Rather, they all go on to specify that belief in God: "I believe in God, the Father. . . . And in Jesus Christ, his Son. . . . And in the Holy Spirit."

Therefore, one task of Christian doctrine is to identify carefully and clearly the God in whom we believe and to whom we have given our lives.

This task may be approached in a number of ways. Some theologians begin in one place, some in another. Some emphasize one way of identifying God, some another. Where a theologian begins does not necessarily reflect what that theologian thinks is most important. As I describe the various possibilities, think about your belief in God and about the theologians with whom you are familiar. Where does the work of identifying God begin? Does our beginning point matter? What is most important for identifying the God in whom Christians believe? Can one thing be more important than another?

The Existence of God

Some theologians begin their doctrine of God by seeking to prove God's existence. These theologians think we must establish the existence of something before we can begin to consider its identifying characteristics. Thomas Aquinas (1225-1274) has been considered a representative of this approach, but recently many students of his work have challenged that traditional understanding of his approach. Unquestionably, however, others represent this approach.

Theologians who begin by establishing the existence of God lay out several arguments for God's existence. These arguments have been given "technical" names, that is, names used as shorthand to remind us of the much longer argument. They go by names like the "ontological argument," the "cosmological argument," and the "teleological argument." These are the most popular, but theologians may add to them other arguments of which they are particularly convinced. The details of the arguments need not concern us here; rather, what is important for us to note is that when a theologian uses them, they represent that theologian's belief that the first thing we must do to identify the Christian God is establish God's existence.

This approach has been criticized by many theologians. After all, these critics ask, don't we need to know what we believe God is like before we argue about whether God exists? Can we begin by arguing that God exists, and after establishing that, argue about what God is like? In a slightly more subtle way, some of these critics argue that proofs for the existence of God sometimes presuppose things about the nature of God that are never examined. In other words, the proofs for the existence of God "smuggle in" particular beliefs about God that are never acknowledged. Thus, some version of the ontological argument may presuppose things about God's character that are never clearly acknowledged or argued. These presuppositions may control the rest of one's doctrine of God in hidden ways.

In contrast to these criticisms, a number of recent studies have argued that although theologians like Thomas Aquinas and Anselm of Canterbury are famous for their arguments for the existence of God, their arguments always presuppose a Christian doctrine of God. Therefore, although they seem to begin with the existence of God, they are not arguing for the existence of some God whose nature is to be specified later; rather, their arguments for the existence of God are arguments for the existence of the God of the Bible who is confessed in the church's creeds.

So we cannot make simple judgments about theologians based on where their doctrine of God begins. We must be wise and discerning readers.

The Attributes of God

Some theologians begin their doctrine of God with a description of God's attributes or characteristics. This approach usually entails a list of the attributes and a definition or description of each attribute. These lists include attributes such as holiness, love, righteousness, mercy, omniscience, omnipotence, infinity, patience, and so on. Although some attributes appear on most lists, theologians usually have their own particular list. This tells us that these lists are not exhaustive descriptions of God; rather, they serve as reminders of God or as pointers to God.

These lists are divided in various ways. Probably the most common is a division between the communicable and incommunicable attributes. This does not mean that God has communicated some attributes to humanity and has not communicated others, at least in the way we typically use the word "communicate." Rather, "communicable" means that some of the characteristics of humanity are also characteristic of God, only to a greater degree. For example, love is something that both God and humans have, only God's love is perfect.

"Incommunicable" means that some attributes of God are not found to a lesser degree in humans. In other words, they are entirely lacking in human beings. For example, to say that God is "infinite" is not to say that God is less finite than humans; rather, it is to say that God is not finite in any way. (Since "infinite" is a negation — "God is 'not finite'" — there is no way to turn this belief around and make it a positive statement.)

We can understand this distinction better by thinking of the commands of the Bible. Since love is an attribute shared to a greater or lesser degree by God and humankind, it makes sense for us to be commanded to love as God loves. And by God's grace we can love as God loves. But nowhere in Scripture are we commanded to be infinite as God is infinite. Such an attainment is impossible for humans.

Another way of dividing a list of God's attributes, made popular by Karl Barth, is to divide it into attributes of God's freedom and attributes of God's love. In this division the former roughly correspond to the incommunicable attributes, and the latter to the communicable attributes.

Barth's division may be taken as one way of responding to criticisms that were directed toward the communicable-incommunicable division. This division and the listing of attributes, the critics said, often tended to be impersonal. Some might go so far as to say that this approach is inevitably impersonal. That is, it seems to be identifying God as the sum total of these attributes, or what we get when we mix together these ingredients. Extending this criticism, some critics argue that the communicable-incommunicable approach detaches our doctrine of God from Scripture and makes God a concept that we define.

Although we can learn from these criticisms, we may at the same time give a more positive evaluation of this approach to the doctrine of God. We may regard more positively the listing and describing of God's attributes if we regard them as reminders of the biblical revelation of God and the church's reflection on that revelation.

Perhaps we can better understand this through a crude illustration. You may be familiar with some form of the story about a bar where all the regulars have heard each other's jokes so often that they no longer tell a joke. Instead they have assigned numbers to all the familiar jokes, so that when someone wants to tell a joke he or she simply calls out the number. Everyone then recalls the joke and laughs. A visitor to the bar one night catches on to what is happening and, wanting to participate in the fun, calls out, "Number five." No one laughs, and one of the regulars remarks, "The guy just doesn't know how to tell a joke."

In an admittedly crude way, this story represents what we are doing when we rehearse the attributes or recall one particular attribute of God. In listing and describing these attributes, we are rehearsing or recalling what God has done and who God is revealed to be by those actions, whether our recollection is stated positively ("God is love") or negatively ("God is not finite"). This means, then, that we must evaluate any account of the attributes of God by their ability to recall for us who God is. What matters in the end, however we organize a list of attributes and whatever we include in our list, is whether our account is faithful to the biblical account and the church's reflection.

Another possible difference in the way theologians identify God may arise as we seek to identify the God in whom Christians believe. This difference could be treated as a separate issue, but I think it may be better understood if we consider it as a part of my discussion of the attributes. This difference is represented by the terms *via negativa, via affirmativa,* and *via eminentia,* which mean "way of negation," "way of affirmation," and (more awk-wardly) "way of enlargement" respectively.

These three ways may be used to describe how we arrive at various attributes of God, but they may also represent more fundamental differences in theological accounts of the doctrine of God. Used of the attributes, they may simply distinguish how we state an attribute. So, for example, when we say that God is infinite, we have used the *via negativa* (to say that God is "not finite"); when we say that God is love, we have used the *via affirmativa* (to affirm the attribute of God's love); when we say that God is omnipotent, we have used the *via eminentia* (to say that God is more than powerful, God is "all-powerful").

Used to identify a more fundamental difference in how theologians approach the doctrine of God, these ways raise a more subtle and difficult-to-resolve problem. For example, some theologians use the *via negativa* to characterize all our talk about God. Such theologians argue that all we can do to identify God is say what or who God is not. Even our apparently affirmative statements about God are at bottom statements about what God is not or does not do.

Since we live in an age that stores a lot of confidence in the human ability to know, this way of thinking may seem strange and unacceptable. But we should also recognize that it has a long history of acceptance in the church and many perceptive advocates today.

By way of contrast, theologians who follow the *via affirmativa* argue that we can in fact make statements about God that actually identify what and who God is. They do not exclude statements of negation, such as "God is not finite," but they add to them the belief that they also tell us something about who God is.

The differences between these approaches are too complex and difficult for me to resolve here. In fact, my discussion has merely attempted to alert you to their existence and to give you a very brief introduction to them. Nevertheless, at the very least we should learn from them something about our own character as theologians. From the advocates of the *via negativa* we should learn to attach an appropriate humility to our statements about God. And from the advocates of the *via affirmativa* we should learn to attach an appropriate confidence to the Bible, the church's tradition, and the power of the Spirit to guide us.

Hidden in the midst of this discussion of the attributes of God (until now) is the question of how we use language to refer to God. This leads us to the difficult issue of *analogy*. Analogy is a concept developed by theologians to guide our understanding of how language refers to God. To help you understand the issues, I will begin with an image and then give you an explanation. Look at the image below, and without thinking about it too much, say out loud what it is:

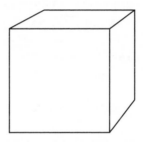

When I draw this image on the blackboard in my classroom and ask my students what it is, most of them say it is a cube. After thinking for a moment, they realize that it is not a cube. It is merely a two-dimensional representation of a three-dimensional reality. But for all its limitations, we still recognize that the artist (if I may use the term) is using the material at hand to refer to a cube. This exercise may help us understand the analogical use of language in contrast to other uses.

In contrast to analogy, we could think of the use of language to refer to God as *univocal*. In this understanding language would refer to God in exactly the same way it refers to humans. This would be like insisting that the drawing on the board really is a cube. In other words, a univocal approach to language about God would insist that our words are identical with God's reality.

In contrast, we could think of the use of language to refer to God as *equivocal*. In this understanding language used of God would have no connection to its use by humans. This would be like saying that the figure on the board tells us nothing about anything but itself. In other words, an equivocal approach to language about God would insist that our words tell us nothing about God.

Faced with these difficulties, theologians have argued that language about God is *analogical*. That is, in spite of the limitations of language and the fact that our words are not identical to God's reality, our language really does tell us something about God.

Analogy, then, is a concept crucial to the Christian doctrine of God. At one level it is elegant in its simplicity. But it also has depths and complexities that invite reflection beyond the purpose of this introduction. For that reason alone, theology is a practice that can engage our intellectual abilities for a lifetime.

Stories and Images

Recently, some theologians pointed out that although the Bible does include celebration of the attributes of God (for example, Exod. 34:6; Ps. 25:8, 10; 1 John 4:9; and many others), the dominant way of identifying God in the Bible is through stories and images. Although this insight has not yet been incorporated into many theologies, we may see more and more of it in time.

Theologians who pursue this approach argue that telling stories is one of the primary ways that we identify one another. For example, if I am telling one friend about another friend, a physical description may help. But to really know someone, to know who a person is, we remember and tell stories. If I want others to know that a friend of mine is caring and compassionate, I may use those words, but I will also add a story about how that friend went for a long walk with me when I was discouraged.

In the same way, some stories of the Bible tell us better than anything else what we mean when we say that God is loving, or merciful, or holy. Of the many lectures on theology that I have heard, the one I remember most vividly is the retelling of the story of Jacob by Thomas Langford. At the end of that story-lecture, I knew better than ever before what it meant to say that God is merciful. From that lecture I learned to look for other biblical stories that identify the character of the God in whom we believe. Of course, among the most memorable for all of us are the parable-stories of Jesus.

These theologians would further argue that stories not only connect well with the way we talk about one another, they also identify God's actions better than concepts do. In other words, they identify God as a personal agent. This argument depends upon the insight that a person's actions are identified by a narrative. Concepts identify an agent — one who acts — only by reference to those actions. A person may rightly be described as "funny" only if it refers to actions by her that we regard as "funny," such as telling a joke, making witty comments, or playing a practical joke. Concepts, therefore, cannot be substitutes for actions when they refer to a personal agent; instead, they must be reminders of those actions. Furthermore, some theologians argue, we need to recapture the reality to which our concepts refer by giving greater attention to the stories of God. (By the way, this may be why people enjoy learning theology more from the stories of someone like C. S. Lewis than from theological textbooks — like this one!)

Some theologians have begun pointing out that images also play a dominant role in biblical talk about God. Here are just a few images that the Bible contains: shepherd, king, savior, warrior, rock, shield, fortress, and vine. Theologians who advocate greater attention to these and other images argue that attending to biblical images forces us to incorporate the ordinary stuff of our lives into our doctrine of God. By so doing God becomes more than someone who exists, more than a list of concepts; God becomes woven into the fabric of our everyday lives.

Since theology has tended in recent history to be dominated

by conceptual thinking, theologians have attended more to concepts than to stories and images in developing a doctrine of God. Conceptual thinking may have the advantage of clarity and precision, but it may also run the risk of becoming lifeless. Renewed attention to the stories and images of the Bible, for which some theologians are calling, may help our theology regain vitality and connection to our everyday lives.

Trinity

One of the most significant recent developments in theology is the large amount of attention being given to the doctrine of the Trinity. Although Christians confess this doctrine, most of us would have difficulty saying what it means or what connection it has to our lives. Since this doctrine is central to our faith, we should welcome this renewed attention to it. And as the work of "professional" theologians filters down to "lay" theologians, we should look forward to its impact on the church.

Most theologians who have led this renewal of reflection on the doctrine of the Trinity also argue that it is the key to the Christian doctrine of God. For this reason they also argue that it should be the first thing we say as Christians about God. Or at least, that it is the most important thing we have to say about God.

In other words, for these theologians the doctrine of the Trinity distinguishes our belief in God from other ways of believing in God. Think back to the beginning of this chapter, where I observed that many traditions confess belief in God and asked whether Christians, Moslems, and Jews all believe in the same God. If we understand that Christians always refer to the Trinity when we confess belief in God, then we can see that Christians, Moslems, and Jews do not all believe in the same God. Already we can begin to see the practical significance of the doctrine of the Trinity.

To understand this further, we may consider the close connection between the doctrine of the Trinity and our Christology, that is, our beliefs about Jesus Christ. The connection between these two beliefs is demonstrated by the fact that the early church worked out these two doctrines simultaneously. From about A.D. 125 (shortly after the completion of the books that constitute our New Testament) until 451 (when church leaders gathered and produced a statement at the Council of Chalcedon), the church struggled to establish the boundaries for the proper language to use about God and Jesus Christ.

In the next chapter we will consider Christology; here we are concerned with the Trinity. During these early years of its existence (125-451), the church labored to develop a doctrine of God that could also account for the significance of what occurred in Jesus Christ. We believe that in Jesus Christ God became human. We also believe that Jesus Christ was sent by the Father. What, then, does this do to our belief in one God? And when we add to this the statements of the New Testament that place the Holy Spirit on a level with the Father and Jesus Christ, the question becomes more difficult. Do we believe in three Gods or one?

The church refused to answer the question in the way that I have stated it. Since the early church understood that God who came in Jesus Christ is the God of the Old Testament, the church refused to surrender the oneness of God. At the same time, the church also refused to surrender belief in the divinity of Jesus Christ and the Holy Spirit. As a result, the church arrived at the doctrine of the Trinity: God is three and one.

When we reflect further on this history, we can see that the doctrine of the Trinity is not an abstract idea made up by some professional theologians to confuse the church. Rather, the doctrine is a response to the revelation of God in Jesus Christ and the coming of the Holy Spirit that guides us in many ways. For example, the doctrine of the Trinity teaches us to read the Old and New Testaments as one story: the God of the Old Testament is also the God of the New Testament. The doctrine also guides our understanding of the good news of Jesus Christ: God has come to us in Jesus Christ. Moreover, it teaches us that today

God is present in the Holy Spirit. These examples certainly do not exhaust the significance of the doctrine of the Trinity. In your own study of theology you should be able to add other examples to these.

This brief historical reflection should help you begin to recognize the significance of the doctrine of the Trinity. But before we move on to other trinitarian issues, I should register one warning. Although the creeds of the church are trinitarian in their shape, none of them teaches us to confess the Trinity. The point I am making here is a subtle but important one. All the creeds are trinitarian in their shape. That is, they reflect the oneness and threeness of God: "I believe in God, the Father . . . and in the Son . . . and in the Holy Spirit." But none confesses, "I believe in the Trinity." Not all theologians are agreed on the significance of this point, but perhaps the best way to understand it is to recognize that the doctrine of the Trinity is a rule for the way we believe in God. That is, it represents what we mean when we confess that we believe in the Father, Son, and Holy Spirit.

As we reflect on how the church came to understand God as Trinity, another issue arises: When we speak of God as Trinity, are we referring to God's internal life, the relations of the Father, Son, and Holy Spirit to one another, or are we referring to God's external relations, how God revealed Godself to us? Theologians refer to these as the "immanent" and the "economic" Trinity. Here "immanent" refers to God's being as Father, Son, and Holy Spirit in relation to one another. "Economic" refers to the work of God the Father, Son, and Holy Spirit in creation and redemption. How the immanent and economic Trinity relate to one another has been a topic of debate among theologians. Two issues are at stake in this complex but important debate. One issue is God's freedom. If the immanent and economic Trinity are identical, then God is not acting freely in creation and redemption. The other issue is God's revelation of who God is. If the immanent and economic Trinity are separated, then we do not truly know God through God's work. The trick in the midst of many complicated conceptual issues is to maintain the proper balance between God's being and God's doing.

Another question that leads us further into the doctrine of the Trinity asks where we should begin our reflections on God as Trinity. Do we begin with God's oneness or God's threeness? One way of answering this question arose in the "Western" theological tradition that developed in European civilizations; this is the tradition most familiar to Catholics and Protestants. Theologians in this tradition begin their doctrine of the Trinity with God's oneness. Beginning with God's oneness may lead to certain emphases in our doctrine of God. We may be likely to think of God as a monarch; we may emphasize God's majesty. This approach may also bring particular difficulties. We may tend to emphasize the divinity of one of the Godhead, either the Father, the Son, or the Holy Spirit. Or we may tend to deny the divinity of the three. In the West this tendency has sometimes led to Unitarianism — the denial of the divinity of the Son and the Holy Spirit. We are not wrong when we begin with the oneness of God, but we should be aware of the potential errors we face.

Another theological tradition, with which most of us are unfamiliar, begins with the threeness of God. This is the "Eastern" theological tradition that developed in the eastern Mediterranean and that is represented today by the various branches of the Eastern Orthodox church, such as the Greek, Syrian, and Russian Orthodox Churches. By beginning with the threeness of God, this theological tradition emphasizes different aspects of God than the Western tradition does. For example, this approach may lead to an emphasis on the sociality of God rather than on God's monarchy. But like the Western tradition, the Eastern theological tradition may also lead to error. For example, some Western theologians are concerned about the way Eastern theologians describe the relationship between the Father and the Son. In the Eastern tradition there may be a tendency to shift monarchy from God as Trinity to the Father alone. When the Eastern tradition begins to think of the Father as monarch,

Western theologians worry that this subordinates the Son and the Spirit to the Father in erroneous ways.

This leads to a further question about the Trinity that reveals the most significant division between the Eastern and Western traditions: Where do we locate the unity of the Father, Son, and Holy Spirit? That is, when we say "Father, Son, and Holy Spirit," the threeness of God is evident. Where then is the oneness of God? In the West the oneness of God is located in the one substance of God, or in confessing that God is one being. In the East the oneness of God is located in the Father, who sends the Son and the Spirit. We might picture the difference this way:

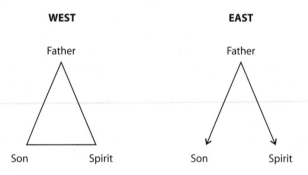

This difference is reflected in two versions of the Nicene Creed. In the East, one line in the last part (or article) of the creed reads, "[I believe] in the Holy Spirit, who proceeds from the Father." In the West, this line has an added clause: "[I believe] in the Holy Spirit, who proceeds from the Father *and from the Son.*" This addition is called the *filioque* (from the Latin for "and the Son"). The details of the historical controversy over this addition do not concern us here, though we may note that this controversy was a major factor in the Great Schism of the Eastern and Western Church in 1054. For our purposes the theological significance is this: to the Eastern tradition the addition of this clause destroys the unity of God. With the confession that the Spirit proceeds from the Father *and from the Son,* the picture of God now looks like this to the Eastern tradition:

Since the Eastern tradition does not primarily conceive of the unity of God as one of substance or being, this Western version of the Nicene Creed has so far proven to be an insurmountable barrier to reconciliation between the Eastern and Western Church.

At the same time, however, in front of this seemingly insurmountable barrier, one of the liveliest theological conversations is taking place. This is happening as several Western theologians develop their trinitarian doctrine by drawing on the insights of the Eastern theological tradition. For many centuries these traditions have developed in isolation from one another. Today, we can find serious consideration of the Eastern tradition in the work of Western theologians. And we may look forward in the coming decades to further rapprochement.

In addition to whether to begin with God's threeness or oneness, theologians are raising other questions about the doctrine of the Trinity. The early church wrestled with which words in Greek could be used to represent the oneness and threeness of God. Today, one of the most significant questions concerns our use of the word "person." Many Christians are familiar with using this word in relation to the Trinity because of the last line of the hymn "Holy, Holy, Holy," where we sing, "God in three persons, blessed Trinity!" Although no theologians have suggested that we change the words of this wonderful hymn, some have raised questions about our understanding today of the word "person" when used about the Trinity. When the Latin word *personae* was first used of the threeness of the Trinity, it had a meaning much different from the meaning of the word "person" today. Unlike in the original Latin, the word "person" is today nearly synonymous with "individual." Although this may seem like theological hairsplitting, it has serious implications for our belief in God. If we think of a person as an individual, and we think of God as three persons, aren't we coming close to thinking of God as three individual Gods? At the very least, this theological reflection teaches us the need to be vigilant in our language for God and to be particularly thoughtful about our use of "God in three persons." Perhaps we should always remind ourselves that we don't mean that the Father, Son, and Holy Spirit are persons in the same way that the author and readers of this book are persons. And as we will see in our chapter on the Christian doctrine of humanity, this may also cause us to think more carefully about human beings as "persons."

This section on the doctrine of the Trinity should whet your appetite for more theological reflection on this doctrine. It is an eminently practical doctrine, developed by the church in its reflection on the good news of salvation through Jesus Christ. Theologians who are leading the renewal of interest in this doctrine have much to teach us about God and the Christian life.

Two Issues

Some recent challenges to our traditional way of doing theology have made two issues particularly pertinent to the doctrine of God: (1) the use of male and masculine language for God, and (2) the significance of our social location. It is important for us to note that the theologians who raise these challenges are not, for the most part, challenging God. Rather, they are challenging our *understanding* of God, asking whether we are using proper language and concepts to guide our understanding and our life as Christians.

The issue of male and masculine language for God arises from feminist theologies. (We should observe that not all feminist theologians are women and not all women theologians are feminist theologians. We should also note that feminist theology has tended to be produced by white people and has been challenged by womanist theologies done primarily by African American women and *mujerista* theologies done primarily by Latina theologians.) As we will note in later chapters, feminist theologies have implications for many Christian doctrines. On the doctrine of God, they have focused attention on our use of male language and masculine images and concepts.

For example, when we say that God is "Father," in what sense do we mean that? When we describe a human male as a "father," we typically mean that he has a child as a result of sexual intercourse. Obviously, we do not mean this when we call God "Father." Nor do we mean that God the Son is the result of sexual intercourse between the Father and a female consort, human or otherwise. (It may be significant here that Mary conceives the human Jesus by the work of the Holy Spirit, not by the Father.) Furthermore, when we call one of the Trinity "Father" and another "Son," are we implying that they are male? In what sense would they be male? We certainly don't mean that they have male sexual organs. Christians believe that God is spirit; God does not have a body.

(In this regard we need to think carefully about Jesus Christ. Certainly in his humanity Jesus was a male. But as hard as it is for us to grasp it, this does not mean that God became a male. In fact, nowhere in the New Testament do we read that God became "a male" or that God became "a man." Rather, the New Testament and much of the theological tradition is careful to say that God became flesh [the "Word became flesh," John 1:14] or that God became human.)

So, feminist theologies challenge us to reconsider the meaning of "male" language for God. They also challenge us to recon-

sider our masculine concepts of God. For example, when we say
that God is strong, do we mean that God is strong like men, able
to run faster and lift heavier objects than women can? Or do we
mean that God is strong like women, healthier in old age and living longer than men? When we think of the love of God, do we
think of it in the way we think of men's love in our culture, or in
the way we think of women's love in our culture? In a similar
manner, feminist theologies question our use of masculine imag-
ery for God. Certainly, the Bible uses masculine images for God,
but the Bible also uses feminine images for God. Has our theological tradition been so male-dominated that we have neglected
the feminine images? As hard as it is for many of us, these questions should cause us to look at the biblical revelation and reconsider our understanding of God.

These are difficult questions, surrounded today by a lot of
theological controversy. Theologians consider them to varying
degrees in their work. For some theologians, these questions are
the heart of the theological task and dominate their work. For
others they are important but not dominant. For still others,
they are peripheral to the work of theology. And for some they
have little or no bearing on the work of theology.

Theologians who consider these questions raised by feminist theologies answer them in different ways. Some consider
them only to show how wrong they are. Others seek to incorporate feminist insights into their theology by revising the tradition at various points. Some of these use traditional language but remind us that we should not think of God as male
or masculine. Others revise the language of the doctrine of
God. So, for example, they speak of God as Father-Mother, or
simply as Mother. Or they revise the language for the Trinity,
and speak of God as Parent, Child, and Spirit. Other feminist
theologians conclude that the Bible and Christianity are so patriarchal that the tradition must be rejected entirely. These
theologians typically do not think of themselves within the
Christian tradition any longer and may call for "Goddess"
worship in place of traditional Christian worship. As you can

imagine, these changes cause considerable controversy and criticism.

Whatever your reaction is to these various responses to the feminist challenge to the tradition, you should not let it obscure the important questions that have been raised. These questions are now part of the life of the church. Anyone who has the privilege of studying theology also has the responsibility to consider them carefully.

Another issue receiving increasing attention in the doctrine of God is the impact of our social location on the way doctrine develops. This issue has been pressed upon us by liberation theology, a movement that began among Christians in Latin America in the 1960s and has since spread to other parts of the world. Some European and North American theologians reject liberation theology as anti–North American and anticapitalist; others reject it for doctrinal reasons; still others adopt it wholeheartedly; and some make limited use of it. Whatever one ultimately concludes about liberation theology, it has raised a significant issue for the doctrine of God that we must seek to understand.

As a result of the work of liberation theology, more theologians are paying attention to the role of social location in shaping a doctrine of God. For example, the early church, arising within the social context of Greek philosophy, paid a lot of attention in their doctrine of God to "metaphysical" questions, including the language we use for God's threeness and oneness, the tension between claiming that God is present everywhere in the world but is not identical with the world, and the question of God's relation to time. In the Greek culture to which the church proclaimed the gospel, these were important questions to address. But liberation theology has forced us to consider whether these are the only important questions, or the most important questions for all cultures. And most significantly, liberation theology has argued that these issues may obscure, and often have obscured, the biblical revelation of God.

Consider, for example, the situation of the poor Christian believer in a Latin American country where Christianity is the faith claimed by a vast majority of the population. As long as the doctrine of God is dominated by traditional metaphysical issues, God is going to have little relevance to the poor believer's life. In this situation liberation theology challenges the theological tradition to take another look at the Bible to see that God works on behalf of the poor and oppressed. Thus, far from being irrelevant to the peasant's life, God is directly involved.

Latin American liberation theologians agree in many ways, but they also have differences. Some attack the traditional doctrine of God for obscuring the true nature of God and distorting the good news of Jesus Christ for the poor and oppressed. Others accept that metaphysical questions were appropriate to Greek culture, even though they have little relevance to circumstances of oppression and injustice today. But all are agreed that the biblical story of God, exemplified by texts such as Exodus 3:7-10, Deuteronomy 10:18, Luke 1:51-53, and 4:18-19, reveals that God is the liberator of the poor and oppressed.

Not all theologians directly engage the questions of liberation theology. But many are at least wrestling with the influence of our social location on the development of the doctrine of God. This question is pertinent in all cultures, but to bring it clearly into focus, we will consider its relation to the church in the United States. One "social location" that is particularly pertinent and often painful for Christians in the United States is race. Given the history of slavery, segregation, and racism, questions in this area are difficult to ask and to hear. African American theologians, who draw on a rich legacy of Christian belief and practice, challenge us to consider whether in the traditional doctrine of God we have a God who is "white."

The question African American theologians ask is about the nature of our concept of God. Here "white" and "black" denote social locations that are dependent upon racial identity. So these theologians challenge us to recognize that we live in a society in which "whites" have been masters and have profited from an order built upon the dominance of one race by another. Have we, as a result, developed a doctrine of God that portrays God on the side of the powerful, a God who sustains social order, even when it is unjust? Like Latin American liberation theologians, they challenge us to recover the biblical teaching that God is on the side of the poor, the powerless, and the oppressed. They challenge us to recognize that God disrupted the Egyptian social order by freeing the Israelite slaves; that God disrupted Israelite society by sending them away into exile in part because of their treatment of the widows, the orphans, and the poor; and that God in Jesus Christ blesses the poor and judges their oppressors.

Again, these issues may be found to varying degrees among theologians. If they are not directly addressed by particular theologians, you should consider whether their work is open to these issues, whether it needs correction, or whether they may have implicitly incorporated some of these insights. In particular, you should consider the role that sex, class, and race play in a theological work. For some theologians, their theology is an expression of experience rooted in sex, class, or race. In other words, theology is a religious interpretation of their experience as a man or woman, privileged or underprivileged, Caucasian or African American. For others, their experience gives them a perspective from which to look at the Bible and the church's tradition that may enable them to see things that others have missed. In other words, theology is an interpretation of the Bible and the church's tradition that is influenced by our social location.

In the first case, experience is authoritative and doctrine is an expression of that experience. When such theologians encounter a biblical passage that runs counter to their experience, then that portion of the biblical text is judged to be outdated, irrelevant, or oppressive, and it is discarded. In the second case, the biblical text is authoritative for interpreting experience. When such theologians encounter a biblical passage that seems to conflict with their experience, they may seek to conform their understanding of their experience to the text, but they often also look for other biblical teaching to which they subordinate the difficult passage.

For example, Paul's letters sometimes instruct slaves to be

faithful and obedient to their masters. Is this a biblical affirmation of slavery? Theologians who take the first approach to theology will answer yes and discard the passage. Theologians who take the second approach will point to passages where Paul instructs masters to treat their slaves well and to passages in Paul and elsewhere in the Bible that teach that all are created equal and that all are equal in Christ. These are the passages that motivated the Christians who led the fight to abolish slavery and the slave trade.

Obviously, the issues raised by feminist, liberation, and African American theology are difficult. They must be addressed ultimately not by a theological system but by living relationships. For this reason, they are usually more painful and difficult than questions about organizing God's attributes or about the place of arguments for God's existence. But for this reason they are also important for theological work that guides our lives and our witness.

Conclusion

Although many Christians faithfully confess belief in God without ever considering the issues I have raised, the church needs some whose calling is to think about such matters. Questions and challenges that call for careful thinking continually arise both inside and outside the church. These questions are difficult and call for the very best in us. We typically admire the intellectual abilities and accomplishments of those who understand the intricacies of physics. Physics, however, is only the study of the world that God has created. Theology is the study of God, who is creator and redeemer. Therefore, even with the revelation of God in Scripture and the guidance of the Holy Spirit, we should not be surprised that the work of theology calls for the very best that we have to give. And we should be thankful for the theologians we study, who have gone before us to understand the God in whom we believe.

CHAPTER 3

The Person of Jesus Christ

When we come to the study of Jesus Christ, we come to the heart of Christian doctrine, wherever theologians may place it in their work. After all, Jesus Christ is what ultimately makes Christian doctrine *Christ*ian. In this chapter and the next, we consider together the way theology guides faithful thinking and living in relation to Jesus Christ.

Why do we have two chapters on Jesus Christ? There is an obvious practical reason: because Jesus Christ is such a big topic that dividing our study in two makes it more manageable. But there is also a theological reason. Traditionally, theology has divided the study of Jesus Christ into a concern for who he is (the person of Christ) and what he did (the work of Christ). The study of the person of Christ is often called Christology, though sometimes that term can be used in a broader sense for everything about Jesus Christ. The study of the work of Christ usually focuses on his crucifixion and resurrection.

In this chapter we are concerned with the person of Christ; in the next chapter we will consider his work. But before we begin we will note two things about this division of person and work.

First, we should note that dividing our study in this way can mislead us into separating the person from his work. But we cannot really have one without the other. Our understanding of who Jesus is must shape our understanding of what he did; and what

35

he did must shape our understanding of who he is. The person and the work go together. Some theologians today are challenging us both to rethink this separation between the person and the work and to find ways of overcoming it.

Second, we should note what we often leave out when we study the person, crucifixion, and resurrection of Jesus Christ, and that is any study of his life. To be sure, we draw on what he said and did to demonstrate his humanity and to show his own claims to divinity. Moreover, his crucifixion and resurrection are part of his life. But often Christian doctrine is concerned to show only *that* he was human, not *how* he was human. We give evidence for the claim *that* he lived a human life, but we do not consider *how* he lived that life.

Of course, if theology is concerned with the church's teachings about Jesus Christ, we could argue that our doctrine should focus on the church's claims about Jesus Christ, not on his life. Traditionally, most theologians have left the study of Jesus' life to NT scholars. Nevertheless, if one of the purposes of our doctrine is to identify who Jesus Christ is, then surely we should pay more attention to his life and integrate his life — his words and his deeds — into our doctrine. Who he is and what he did for us on the cross are ultimately inseparable from the way he lived. So, keeping in mind the inseparability of the life, the person, and the work of Jesus Christ, let us turn to the study of his person.

The Person of Jesus Christ

The doctrine of Jesus Christ — Christology — consumed most of the theological energy of the early church. As the church pursued its commission to preach the gospel, the hearers of that message naturally asked questions about that gospel focused on Jesus Christ. These questions and the answers proposed in response gave rise to serious reflection on what the gospel claimed about Jesus Christ. The history of this reflection is the place for us to start in our understanding of the concerns of Christology.

Historical Development

The person of Jesus Christ became a doctrinal issue very early in the history of the church. What should the church teach about Jesus Christ? Along with the doctrine of the Trinity, this question and its answer were the focus of the first councils of the church. The church's claims about Jesus Christ became an issue because the church was claiming something strange about him: this one person was both divine and human. How could two natures — divine and human — exist in one person? Indeed, could they? The church, in considering various answers to these questions, did not establish a "bull's-eye" that must always be hit when claims about the person of Jesus Christ are made. Rather, it developed "boundaries" within which Christology must be located. These boundaries establish the limits outside which Christians must not stray if we are to remain faithful in our Christology. As the church established these boundaries, it also identified views that were outside of them and views that were inside of them. Outside views are "heresy," inside views are "orthodoxy."

How could Jesus Christ be two natures in one person? Many answers were proposed. Some solved the apparent contradiction by denying one or the other nature. Gnostics and Docetists denied that Jesus was really human. We are uncertain about the precise relationship between Gnostics and Docetists; their views certainly overlap with one another. It may be best to think of "Gnosticism" as the more comprehensive term and "Docetism" as the term that describes the Gnostics' Christology. Gnostics believed that matter was essentially and irredeemably evil. So God could not have come as a human being in the flesh. Docetists, who take their name from the Greek word for "to appear" or "to seem," argued that Jesus was not really human, he only appeared to be human. The church quickly identified these views as heretical, though, as we will see, some today are questioning this judgment.

In contrast to the denial of Jesus' humanity, another solution to the two natures—one person dilemma is the denial of Jesus' divinity. This view was argued by the Ebionites and Adoptionists. The Ebionites viewed Jesus as the greatest of the prophets sent by God. They viewed Jesus as far superior to other prophets and as the last of the prophets, but they still regarded him as merely human. The Adoptionists argued that Jesus Christ was born as a mere human being but was adopted as God's Son at his baptism. Traditional Christian teaching regards the baptism as a moment when Jesus was *revealed* to be the Son of God; Adoptionists view it as the moment when Jesus *became* the Son of God. Furthermore, they argued that God could not die. Therefore, the divinity of Jesus Christ left him before his death on the cross. Again, the church quickly identified these views as heresy.

The next proposal, however, was not so easily judged. Arius (ca. 260-336) and his followers troubled the church for many years and provoked the first full council of the church after the NT. We do not have many documents written by Arius and his followers, so we must be a bit tentative in our study. It seems clear that Arians argued that true and full divinity does not change or suffer. Therefore, if God became human in Jesus Christ, it must have been a "lesser" divinity that became human in Jesus Christ. This person of the Godhead is the first creature that God made. This "Son" was a creature, through whom the rest of creation was made and who rules over creation. He is capable of change and of suffering because he is a creature.

The views of the Arians were very influential in the early church. But they were vigorously opposed by Athanasius (ca. 296-373). The controversy became so widespread that Emperor Constantine, who had recently made Christianity a "tolerated" religion in the empire, called the leaders of the church together to settle the dispute at the Council of Nicea (325). This council formulated the Nicene Creed. The council decided against the Arians by confessing that Jesus Christ was not similar to God or like God, but, simply, God. He is God just as the Father is God; he has no beginning, he is not part of creation. The Greek word that famously represents the conclusion of the council is *homoousios:* Jesus Christ, in his divinity, is the "same substance" with God.

The controversy, however, did not end with the council. In the following years, at times the Arians dominated the church and at times Athanasius dominated. The controversy was effectively ended at the Council of Constantinople (381). This council not only affirmed the judgments of Nicea, it also revised the Nicene Creed into the form that we say today. In its deliberations and creed it clarified the divinity of the Holy Spirit — something the Council of Nicea had not done. Of special importance to this work were three theologians known as "the Cappadocians." Basil the Great, Gregory of Nyssa, and Gregory of Nazianzus were named for their home province of Cappadocia in Asia Minor. Together they championed the views of Athanasius and extended his arguments about the divinity of the Son to the divinity of the Holy Spirit.

The councils of Nicea and Constantinople effectively established the boundaries for the claim that Jesus Christ is fully human and fully divine. However, within those boundaries was room for different emphases, such as those that developed during the fourth century at two centers for theology, Alexandria in Egypt and Antioch in Syria. At Alexandria the emphasis was placed on Christ's divinity, and at Antioch on his humanity. Most of the theologians at both schools were careful to remain within the boundaries of orthodoxy. But occasionally someone strayed outside the boundaries. Apollinaris (or Apollinarius), a theologian at Alexandria, was judged by the Council of Constantinople (381) to have denied the full humanity of Jesus Christ. And at the Council of Ephesus (431), Nestorius, a theologian from Antioch, was judged to have denied Christ's full divinity. Even with the boundaries set, the mystery of Jesus Christ as fully human and fully divine is not easy to maintain.

In an attempt to resolve these further issues, the leaders of the church met for the Council of Chalcedon (451). That council produced the Chalcedonian Definition of Jesus Christ, which seeks to give further guidelines for faithfulness to the teachings of the earlier councils, especially the Nicene Creed. Even at Chalcedon the church recognized that a final, precise description of Jesus Christ as one person in two natures could not be given. Instead, Chalcedon added more boundary markers. It reaffirmed that the divinity of Jesus Christ is the same divinity as the divinity of the Father, that his humanity is of the same substance as our humanity, and that the humanity and divinity of Jesus Christ are united in the one person, "without confusion, without change, without division or separation."

Still, the controversies continued. Monophysites (Greek, *mono* = one, *physis* = nature) solved the logical conundrum of two natures in one person by arguing that in Jesus Christ the human and divine blended together into a new nature. But the church recognized that this made Jesus neither human nor divine, but a kind of hybrid of the two. Chalcedon had already effectively identified Monophysitism as a heresy. Churches that insisted on holding to Monophysite views separated from the rest of the church. Today, these churches are often identified as Oriental Orthodox churches (Armenian, Coptic, Ethiopian, and Syrian Orthodox), in contrast to Eastern Orthodox churches (a large family of churches such as the Greek, Antiochian, Russian, and other Orthodox churches) that hold to the Chalcedonian Definition. Monothelites (*mono* = one, *thelema* = will) argued that Jesus Christ was fully human and fully divine, but only had a divine will. They did not consider will necessary to full humanity, but at the Third Council of Constantinople (680-81) they were judged to be heretical.

At this point you may be thinking that these controversies seem like a lot of hairsplitting. What is really at stake with all of these careful distinctions? Isn't this history just an instance of intellectuals making too much out of harmless ideas? The early church didn't think so. For the church, what was at stake was the salvation that has come to us in Jesus Christ. The ideas they were wrestling with had very significant practical implications. Underlying their careful judgments were two convictions. First, they were convinced that human beings are incapable of saving themselves; our sin is such that only God could save us. If Jesus Christ was not fully divine, then we are not saved. Second, they were convinced that our full humanity could be redeemed only by God becoming fully human. Only that which God became in Jesus Christ could be redeemed. If Jesus was only partly human, then that part of our humanity that he became was what he redeemed. If Jesus was fully human, then our full humanity is redeemed in Christ. Here we encounter an instance of the ultimate inseparability of Christ's person and work.

In our reflection on and evaluation of these councils, we need to remember that the church was debating among itself the guidelines for its proclamation of the gospel. The creeds are not evangelistic addresses to unbelievers; they are the confessions of the faith of those who have come to belief through the preaching of the gospel. They are not answers to unbelievers but corrections of false doctrine among those who claim to believe.

Contemporary Issues

Today, many, perhaps most, theologians still seek to think about Jesus Christ within the boundaries set by the church councils. Some of these theologians simply seek to restate, explain, and defend the Christology of the councils. Others argue that although we should be careful to remain within the boundaries established by the councils, we must find new language to express our beliefs. These theologians argue that the early church carried on its debate in categories provided by Greek philosophy. For example, the term "substance" (Greek, *ousia*) that formed the basis of the debate between Arius and Athanasius had a very specific meaning in Greek philosophy. Today, the term does not mean much philosophically. Therefore, these theologians argue, we must find new terminology to express the same truths that the councils protected.

In contrast to these contemporary theologians who seek to

remain within the boundaries of the councils, other theologians have questioned those boundaries. Thus, over the last three centuries the issues of Christology have once again become significant in the church. With the rise of the Enlightenment (seventeenth and eighteenth centuries) and its continuing influence, some theologians began to turn away from the authority of the tradition of the church embodied by the church councils and turn toward the authority of human reason. As we have seen, the claim that Jesus Christ is two natures in one person cannot be fully explained. The church councils merely set some boundaries around the mystery. In a quest to remove the mystery and make Christianity "reasonable," some theologians began to question the decisions of the councils.

This quest for "reasonableness" has led some theologians to argue that Jesus Christ was the greatest teacher and example of the way we should live, but that he was not "two natures in one person." This view is tied to other views about sin and salvation that differ from those of the early church. If Jesus is our teacher and example, then he has shown us the way to live so that we may overcome sin and be saved. But this is not the understanding of sin and salvation that marked the Christology of the church councils.

Some who advocate this "modern" view of Jesus Christ argue that he is still the unique Savior because we know the way to live only through his teaching and example. Others argue that this modern view of Jesus means that he is not the unique Savior, but is one among many teachers and examples of the way of salvation.

Many who adopt this view of Jesus support it by arguing that we are no longer bound by the church councils. Like the theologians I noted above, they argue that the councils used the categories of their culture, primarily drawn from Greek philosophy, to develop their Christology. But in contrast to those I noted above, these theologians use that reasoning to set aside the boundaries altogether and argue that the Christology of the early church is metaphorical or symbolic. What we need today are new symbols and metaphors appropriate to the contemporary world. These new symbols and categories are drawn from realms such as contemporary philosophy and psychology and are almost as numerous as theologians.

In the last two centuries another christological belief has arisen that seeks to remain orthodox but give further explanation of the incarnation: "kenotic" (Greek for "emptying") theories. These theories vary in detail but argue in general that to become incarnate in a human being, the second person of the Trinity "emptied" himself. The problem these theories seek to explain is this: How can the infinite, glorious second person of the Trinity become one with a finite, inglorious human being? They answer this question by arguing that God the Son voluntarily limited his divine powers to become incarnate. They base their argument in part on Philippians 2:7, where Paul says Jesus "emptied himself" *(ekenosen,* based on the Greek word *kenosis).* The interpretation of this verse is disputed. Some think it refers to Christ's life of sacrifice after the incarnation, not to a "metaphysical" act that precedes his incarnation. Nevertheless, kenotic theories of the incarnation continue to be discussed and debated today.

Closely related to kenotic theories is the claim that if Jesus Christ is fully divine, then in some sense we must speak of God crucified. Jürgen Moltmann has been a particularly influential advocate of this claim. For him and for others, this claim is tied to the nature of God — that God suffers with us even to the point of death. This view runs contrary to the dominant view in the early church, that God does not suffer. For this reason some reject the claim of Moltmann; but others have found it to be true to the teaching of the Bible and still within the boundaries of orthodoxy.

Another area of controversy today involves a reconsideration of Gnosticism. In the twentieth century we discovered many Gnostic texts that lay buried for many centuries. These discoveries have led a few theologians to argue that politics played a larger role than theology in the condemnation of the Gnostics. In other words, the leaders of the early church condemned Gnosticism to consolidate their power and silence troublemakers, not to establish the truth and safeguard the gospel. Although those wanting to reconsider Gnosticism are active and significant scholars, they are a small minority.

Earlier in this chapter I noted that our usual division of Christology tends to neglect the life of Jesus. One group of theologians calling for renewed attention to Christ's life is liberation theologians. They argue that if we attend to Jesus' life, then we see that his mission in life was to liberate the poor, the oppressed, the marginalized. We considered this theology in the previous chapter, and it will be particularly important in the next chapter, but it also calls us to reconsider our Christology.

One way to put the challenge of liberation theologians is to say that they call us to pay more attention to the political dimension of the person of Jesus Christ. The church councils, in their response to Greek philosophy, primarily dealt with metaphysical issues. Liberation theologians vary in their evaluation of the need to deal with these metaphysical questions, but they all agree that theology has not paid enough attention to the political questions raised by the life of Christ. They also argue that metaphysical questions themselves are also political questions, though we do not often recognize this dimension.

If we pay more attention to the life of Christ, then according to liberation theology we will see that the issue is not simply that Jesus is God and reveals God, but that he reveals the kind of God that God is. God is one who has a special concern for the poor, oppressed, and marginalized. After all, aren't those the ones to whom Jesus carried his message and his mission? He was not concerned with the rich, powerful, and privileged members of society, but with the downtrodden, the outcast, and the powerless. In our Christology, liberation theologians challenge us to go beyond saying that Jesus was fully divine to say that he was fully divine in a particular way revealed by his call to justice. They also argue that he was fully human in a particular way, as one who spent his life with the poor. Since what we believe about Jesus Christ as fully human and fully divine affects the way we live, liberation theologians see their claims as challenges to the church today to live as Christ lived.

Finally, we should note that some theologians, though not heavily influenced by liberation theology, have sought to develop a Christology that brings together the life, person, and work of Jesus Christ. They seek to accomplish this by developing a "narrative Christology." Setting aside the metaphysical debates of the councils, these theologians seek to tell the story of Jesus as the story of one who is fully divine and fully human in his life, death, and resurrection. This christological approach is still being developed and its orthodoxy is being debated. For the most part, these theologians claim to be faithful to the boundaries of orthodoxy while creating new ways of thinking about Jesus Christ.

Conclusion

If God has come to us in Jesus Christ, as the gospel proclaims, then we cannot expect our understanding of that claim to come easily. And we have certainly seen here some of the complexities. At the same time, we have also seen the clear judgments of the church. While there is always mystery in the claim that Jesus Christ is fully human and fully divine, there are also boundaries around that mystery. Some may question those boundaries or set them aside, but the councils of the church have established them. Within those boundaries there has always been room for differences. Some christological reflection today operates within those boundaries, some does not. Making such judgments has never been easy. The early church developed Christology over several centuries. Like them, we must be patient and persistent in our christological reflection, because it stands at the very heart of Christian doctrine. What is always at stake for the church is the faithful passing on of the gospel from one generation to the next. Such faithfulness calls for the very best thinking and living that the grace of God enables in us.

CHAPTER 4

The Work of Jesus Christ

Because Jesus Christ is central to Christianity, it often takes several chapters and topics in a work of theology to cover the doctrines connected to him. In the previous chapter we considered the person of Jesus Christ. In this chapter we will cover two areas of doctrine that are often considered in separate chapters. Even as we consider these topics separately, it is important to remember that they concern one person and his story. Although we may separate them for doctrinal reflection, Jesus' life, person, death, and resurrection are in reality different aspects of the same story.

In the previous chapter I noted the error that theology often makes in neglecting the life of Jesus. Since this is a primer for Christian doctrine, I cannot correct that error here. But I encourage you to think about the relationship between Jesus' death and the way he lived, as well as his resurrection and the way he lived. Was Jesus executed, at least in part, because of the way he lived? And does his resurrection reveal the power of his way of life? These are important questions that are often better addressed in NT studies than in Christian doctrine.

As we consider his death and resurrection, it is also important to remember one even as we consider the other. The Jesus who died is the one who was raised; the Jesus who was raised is the one who died. We cannot think about the significance of his

46

death apart from what his resurrection tells us about his death. And we cannot understand his resurrection apart from the significance of his death. With these warnings in mind, let us consider his death and resurrection.

The Death of Jesus Christ

Christian doctrine has often discussed the death of Christ under the heading "The Work of Jesus Christ." In common usage, "work" can cover a lot of things. When theologians use the term "work" to consider Christ's death, they are identifying the purpose of Christ's coming. They are saying that the significance of Jesus Christ can be located primarily in his death. If Jesus Christ is the center of *Christ*ian doctrine and if his death is at the center of his significance, then we are at the very heart of Christian doctrine when we consider the doctrine of the death of Christ.

Theologians use a variety of terms and categories to develop the doctrine that guides our understanding of Christ's death. "Atonement" is one of the terms many theologians use for this doctrine, even though they may develop it in different ways. "Atonement" derives from the Old Testament system of sacrifices and is used in the New Testament to locate Jesus' death in relation to that system of sacrifice. In a very simple way, we may see the significance of the word by dividing it up: at-one-ment. Atonement is the bringing together of God and humankind through the cross of Jesus Christ.

As theologians reflect on the atonement accomplished by Christ's death, they seek to describe its significance in detail. Their accounts may use concepts, images, themes, or theories to develop in more detail a doctrine of the atonement. I will use three broad categories to prepare you for your study of the atonement. Sometimes one of these categories has been dominant in a particular era or theologian; at other times theologians have sought to give full weight to more than one category. Moreover, though several theologians may use the same broad category for their doctrine, they may develop it in very different ways. The death of Christ is of such significance that no one interpretation will ever exhaust its meaning. After we have some understanding of the different approaches, we will explore them a bit more in comparison with each other.

Three Approaches

One of the earliest categories for interpreting the atonement is _victory_. We may naturally think of Christ's resurrection as a victory, but the NT and Christian doctrine have more often interpreted his death as a victory. In this view Christ's death brings God and humankind together by defeating the powers that separate us. This view was prevalent in the early church, in the writings of Martin Luther (1483-1546), and with several twentieth-century theologians. It is sometimes called the "classical" view of the atonement. Its advocates often emphasize that it is not a "theory" but a "dramatic" view of the atonement. It is also sometimes referred to by a Latin phrase, _Christus Victor._

Early theologians who teach _Christus Victor_ often elaborate on its meaning by using images and language that seem strange to us today. For example, one theologian describes Christ's triumph with the image of bait and a fishhook. Christ's humanity is the bait that drew Satan in; Christ's divinity is the fishhook that destroyed Satan. Similarly, some early theologians use the language of ransom — Christ's death ransomed us. But to whom was the ransom paid? It seems wrong to think of God having to pay a ransom to anyone, such as the devil. When we consider this view of Christ's death as a victory, we are also driven to ask over whom or what was Christ victorious. Theologians have given different answers to this question, among them Satan, death, sin, and the law.

Although there are difficulties in the details of this approach, theologians have found grounds for it in Scripture and in Christian tradition. Today, some theologians have used it to emphasize the structural nature of sin — that sin is found in economic, political, and other social systems. Confronted with poverty, injustice, and oppression, we may find doctrinal guidance from the teaching that Christ's death triumphed over the forces that oppose God and seek to destroy human life.

Another category that theologians have found helpful for developing the doctrine of the atonement is _substitution_. This doctrine emphasizes the conviction that Jesus Christ took our place in death and did something for us that we could not do. Anselm (ca. 1033-1109) developed an account of this doctrine more specifically described as the "satisfaction" theory of the atonement. Drawing on the feudal society in which he lived, Anselm argued that Christ's obedience and death reconciled God and humankind by satisfying the honor of God that we had offended by our disobedience. Later, John Calvin (1509-64) drew on the legal system of his day to argue that Christ suffered the punishment that was due us because of our sins. This view has been developed by a number of theologians as the "penal substitution" view (penal referring to punishment). It is the prevalent doctrine in conservative churches.

This category of substitution emphasizes God's wrath against sin and the punishment for sin that we should receive. Some have questioned this emphasis on God's wrath, especially when this view is developed without reference also to God's love. Nevertheless, if we interpret Christ's death as a sacrifice foreshadowed by OT sacrifices, then the Bible gives some weight to this category of substitution. But as with other doctrines, we must be careful to develop it in appropriate ways. For many theologians this means developing the doctrine of substitutionary atonement in keeping with the Bible and Christian tradition. For others it means using our experience and culture as a guide.

To avoid some of the problems of substitution, some theologians present Christ's atonement as a representation. This is closely connected to substitution, so I will not argue that it is a separate category. But it is a bit different from substitution. On this view Christ did not substitute for us; rather, he represented us before God.

The last category we will consider here is the interpretation of Christ's atonement as *example*. This category was important to Abelard (1079-1142/43), a near contemporary of Anselm. Abelard believed that Anselm's theory placed too much emphasis on God's wrath and not enough on God's love. To counter Anselm, he argued that Christ's death is a demonstration of God's love for sinners, a demonstration so powerful that it can move us to faith in Christ. This view is sometimes labeled the "moral influence" theory, but not everyone agrees that the label is accurate.

After the Enlightenment and the rise of an optimistic view of humankind, other theologians developed Christ's death as an example in a way very different from Abelard. Abelard viewed Christ's death as an example of God's work; these later theologians present it as an example of human work. For them Christ exemplifies what we must achieve as Christians. Friedrich Schleiermacher (1768-1834) argued that Jesus Christ demonstrated what human beings achieve when we are united with Christ by faith.

Now that we have a general outline of these views, we can compare them a bit. The first two views are sometimes called "objective" doctrines of the atonement because they present Christ's atonement as something that took place outside us. The third view is called a "subjective" view because it presents the atonement as something that occurs within us. We may debate the appropriateness of these descriptions, but in the end we must recognize that the atonement occurs outside us, in Christ's death on the cross, and within us, as we come to faith in Christ. The difference in the views lies in the relative emphasis that each places on concepts like wrath and love, on the nature of sin, and on the inner and outer work of Christ.

The views of Christ as victor, substitute, and example of God's love rest on biblical foundations. Schleiermacher and those who present similar views depend less on biblical support. Indeed, their views arise within a context where the authority of the Bible is subordinate to experience and culture. For them the belief that God is wrathful belongs to earlier cultures, not to our own. Therefore, for Christ's death to have significance today, it must be interpreted in ways acceptable to our culture.

In the end each of these views, with the exception perhaps of those like Schleiermacher's, gives us a window into the significance of Christ's death as atonement for our sins. That event stands at the heart of Christian doctrine and continues to have the power to save all who believe. The atonement is of such significance that it defeats our ability to exhaust its meaning and significance. But the study of Christian doctrine helps prepare each generation to be faithful in its witness to the good news of Jesus Christ.

The Extent of the Atonement

One of the historic controversies in Christian doctrine concerns the extent of the atonement. In the sixteenth century John Calvin argued that Christ died only for those whom God had already chosen for salvation. This doctrine of particular or limited atonement is intertwined with other aspects of Calvin's theology, such as predestination (God's sovereign determination of who will be saved) and unconditional election (God chooses who will be saved apart from any action on their part — without condition). Although many today find it difficult to accept, this doctrine was dominant in most Protestant theology after Calvin. Calvin gave it a strong biblical foundation and logical argument, and many conservative theologians continue to teach it.

Shortly after Calvin's death, his doctrine of limited atonement and related doctrines were questioned by James (or "Jacobus") Arminius, a Dutch theologian. Arminius argued that the atonement was general or universal, not particular or limited, though only those who come to faith in Christ receive its benefits. Later, John Wesley (1703-1791) also taught a general atonement. Today, churches continue to differ in their teachings on this question.

We should be careful to note that belief in a "universal" atonement does not necessarily imply belief in universal salvation. (We will return to this in the chapter on the doctrine of salvation.) For Arminius and Wesley the atonement is universal in its scope but not in its application. Only those who believe in Christ benefit from his atonement and are saved. To avoid misunderstanding, Arminian and Wesleyan theologians often describe the atonement as "general" rather than "universal."

Today, one other question about the "extent" of the atonement is often discussed in Christian doctrine. Faced with unjust political and economic structures and the environmental crisis, some theologians argue that we need to recognize the "cosmic" extent of the atonement. They argue that the dominant doctrine of the atonement in conservative theology — substitution — tends to limit the atonement to individuals. As a correction, they teach that the atonement extends beyond individuals to social structures and the entire creation. As I noted above, these theologians tend to draw more on Christ as victor than on Christ as substitute.

The debate between Calvinists and Arminians has been going on for centuries. It is unlikely that we will ever resolve it. Sometimes the argument centers on the interpretation of biblical passages, sometimes on larger doctrinal issues. In the end, I believe that both groups can agree on practical issues: the church should preach the gospel to everyone; salvation is by grace, not works; assurance of salvation is possible; and holiness is essential to Christian living. In the meantime, the theological differences remind us that God is greater than our systems of doctrine.

The Resurrection of Jesus Christ

The good news of Jesus Christ does not end with his death. His story continues to his resurrection and, as we will see in a later chapter, his return. For many Christians the most important question concerning the resurrection is whether or not it happened. Can we prove it or give evidence for it? That is an important task in Christian theology, but it is more the task of apologetics than doctrine. Apologetics is the theological discipline of answering objections to Christianity and giving proofs for Christian beliefs. The task of doctrinal theology is to explore the meaning and significance of Christian beliefs. Of course, our study of doctrine should also increase our belief as we understand more fully the implications of what we believe. Here I will be concerned primarily with the doctrine of the resurrection. But as I introduce some doctrinal approaches to the resurrection, I will also note the kind of evidence that might be given for it. Probably the most familiar doctrinal view of the resurrection is that it is an event in Jesus' life that occurred in history. As I am describing it here, this view lays primary emphasis on the historicity of the resurrection. It is more concerned to give evidence for its occurrence than to develop its theological significance.

Other theologians, such as Wolfhart Pannenberg (1928-) and Jürgen Moltmann (1926-), affirm the resurrection as a historical event in Jesus' life, but they also seek to develop its theological significance. These theologians often describe it as an eschatological event. "Eschatology" is a theological term used to refer to the events that occur at the end of history. When theologians describe Jesus' resurrection as an eschatological event, they are saying that it reveals to us the end of history ahead of time. It's like reading the last few pages of a mystery novel before you read the book. But there's a difference: knowing the end of the mystery robs it of any sense of adventure. Knowing the goal of history revealed in the resurrection of Jesus Christ calls us to an adventure.

Jesus' resurrection tells us where history and all creation is headed. Pannenberg's understanding of Christ's resurrection as an eschatological event that has already occurred in history leads him to emphasize the historical evidence for the resurrection — such as the empty tomb. Moltmann's understanding of Christ's resurrection as an eschatological event revealing the already-coming kingdom of God leads him to look for evidence for the resurrection in the work of the church on behalf of the poor and oppressed.

Perhaps the greatest Protestant theologian of the twentieth century, Karl Barth (1886-1968), argued that the resurrection is an act of God in space and time that is not accessible or subject to historical investigation. He argued that the only evidence we need to give is the teaching of the Bible. Barth was by no means a biblical literalist, but he saw a great gulf between the Bible and modern culture. Confronted with this gulf, he always sought to subordinate modern culture to the Bible. Since the resurrection is an act of God, it also requires an act of God — the gift of faith — to believe the resurrection and have our lives transformed by it. For Barth, the giving of historical evidence for the resurrection was an unacceptable reliance on human reason where reliance on God is called for.

In sharp contrast to Barth is the position of Rudolf Bultmann (1884-1976), an NT scholar and theologian. Bultmann believed that the resurrection is a historical event that occurred in the disciples' lives, not in Jesus' life. After the death of Jesus, the disciples found that the memory of Jesus and his call to discipleship continued to have power for them. In a premodern, unscientific world, "resurrection" was the best, most compelling description they had for this continuing significance of Jesus. However, according to Bultmann, modern people cannot believe in life after death — in a literal, physical resurrection. So, reinterpreting the NT according to modern culture, Bultmann and others argue that the "resurrection" occurs whenever people put their faith in Jesus Christ. Bultmann's doctrine may be described as a psychological or existential view of the resurrection. Bultmann and others who adopt this doctrine also reinterpret many other NT claims in existential categories.

A few theologians go beyond Bultmann by disregarding the resurrection as a topic for Christian doctrine today. It is simply the claim of an earlier view of the world that no longer has relevance for us today. These theologians set aside the authority of the Bible and Christian tradition in favor of their interpretation of contemporary experience.

For most theologians, however, the resurrection of Jesus

Christ remains an integral part of the good news of Jesus Christ that doctrine is called to preserve and guide. Although they may differ at some points on its significance, they agree that without it the story of Jesus is incomplete and "if for this life only we have hoped in Christ, we are of all people most to be pitied" (1 Cor. 15:19).

Conclusion

For most theologians the death and resurrection of Jesus Christ provide the interpretive keys for Jesus' life and for all of God's acts in our world. In Jesus' death we see the willingness of God to enter into our suffering as a sacrifice for sin. In his resurrection we see the power of God to overcome the effects of sin. For some theologians the resurrection is a proof or a sign of Christ's divinity. But it is also a sign of his humanity. When we crucified Jesus Christ, we displayed our verdict — he was a religious blasphemer and political revolutionary. When God raised him from the dead, God reversed our verdict. In the resurrection, God declared that in Jesus we find the true revelation of God and humankind. The life Jesus lived is the life approved by the Giver of life — it is eternal life. The things Jesus taught are true of God and the world. When we are united with Christ by God's gift of faith, his death becomes the end of our old life and his resurrection becomes the source of our new life. May your study of Christian doctrine confirm this truth in your own life given as a sacrifice for others so that you may also know the power of Christ's resurrection (Phil. 3:10-11).

CHAPTER 5

Holy Spirit

At one point in the writing of this primer I debated with myself whether or not to include this chapter on the Holy Spirit. That debate represents the dilemma Christian theology faces in the doctrine of the Holy Spirit: because of the nature and the work of the Holy Spirit, the doctrine of the Holy Spirit seems to be fully treated under other doctrines. Thus, any separate focus on the Holy Spirit seems redundant. As a result, theologies have sometimes given little specific attention to the doctrine of the Holy Spirit. Instead they have treated it as a kind of addition to or aspect of other doctrines. That approach is not entirely wrong, and many theologies do a good job with just such an approach. But treating the Holy Spirit as subordinate to other doctrines may also have the effect of devaluing the Holy Spirit. Some would go further to argue that theology has indeed often neglected and even suppressed the doctrine of the Holy Spirit.

Since I resolved my debate by writing this chapter, you will find some topics here that are also covered in other chapters. In Scripture the Holy Spirit seems to play something of a "supporting role" — enlivening creation, empowering Jesus, transforming humans. In these cases creation, Jesus, and persons are center stage, and the Holy Spirit works through them. But careful thought also reveals that the work of the Holy Spirit plays a central role in the drama. We may even see here the wonderful mystery of the gospel: the work of the Holy Spirit is central, yet that work is for the sake of others.

Thus, some theologians have suggested that Christian theology may be at a point where we should think about what an account of doctrine would look like if the Holy Spirit were regarded as the central figure in the account. But until that suggestion is explored more fully and such an account is actually developed, I will here introduce you to the more traditional approach to the doctrine of the Holy Spirit.

So in this chapter you will note many overlaps with other chapters in this book. That overlap is one of the unavoidable characteristics of the doctrine of the Holy Spirit. But I will also try to bring into focus the doctrine of the Holy Spirit that may be subordinate to other doctrines in some other chapters. This interweaving of doctrines teaches us something about the gospel and the work of theology. A lot of theology is simply looking at the one gospel with different focal points in view. So we learn a lot about God when we look closely at Jesus Christ. We learn about sin when we bring it into focus, but we also learn about sin when we focus on the doctrine of salvation. The doctrine of creation teaches us about humankind, but we also need to focus on humankind as a doctrinal topic. Likewise, in this chapter we will focus on the Holy Spirit in the light of several other doctrines and see how they are interwoven. But I will also try to point out some aspects of this doctrine that are not covered elsewhere in this book. If you read this primer alongside other theologies, you may learn a lot by comparing what is discussed and how it is organized.

The Holy Spirit and God

One crucial aspect of orthodox Christian teaching on the Holy Spirit is the confession of the full divinity of the Spirit, along with the divinity of the Father and the Son. This confession is not always entirely clear to Christians because of the term "Spirit" and because of the nature of the Spirit's work. In some theologies the

Holy Spirit has been referred to as the "shy member" of the Trinity because the Spirit, it is said, likes to stay in the background and work unnoticed. The limited truth in this assertion has sometimes led to the divinity of the Holy Spirit being neglected or even rejected. Further complicating this situation is the scriptural use of the term "spirit" to refer not to the third person of the Trinity but to God's power or God's presence more generally.

We can see the difficulties of this doctrine in the work of the early church. In the creed that was originally confessed by the Council of Nicea, the church just barely confesses belief in the Holy Spirit. After several introductory lines confessing belief in God the Father and many lines confessing belief in God the Son, the original Nicene Creed confesses too briefly, "and we believe in the Holy Spirit." That's all. This relative neglect of the Holy Spirit reflects the nature of the times — the church's teaching on Jesus Christ was under direct assault. And this neglect was corrected at the Council of Constantinople when the Nicene Creed was revised to assert the full divinity of the Holy Spirit: "We believe in the Holy Spirit, the Lord and Life-giver, who proceeds from the Father and together with the Father and the Son is to be worshipped and glorified." One of the Cappadocian Fathers, Basil of Caesarea (also known as Basil the Great), wrote a treatise, *On the Holy Spirit,* which helped the church think through this doctrine carefully. Since that time the great tradition of doctrine has boldly and faithfully confessed the divinity of the Holy Spirit.

When we confess the divinity of the Holy Spirit, we are led quite naturally into the doctrine of the Trinity. The chapter on God considers the doctrine of the Trinity at some length and discusses the role of the doctrine of the Spirit in the split between the church in the East and the West. Here I will focus on one concern regarding the Holy Spirit. In treatments of the Holy Spirit in the doctrine of the Trinity, the Holy Spirit is often regarded as the one who goes between the Father and the Son. These two — the Father and the Son — are easy to differentiate. But identifying the role of the Holy Spirit in the inner life of the

Trinity is not so easy. Many, perhaps most, theologies identify this role in the "gap" between the Father and the Son. The Spirit is the one who unites the Father and the Son; or, the Spirit is the love that goes between them.

This approach is well established in the church's tradition and has much to commend it. But today some theologians are questioning whether such an account of the role of the Spirit really gives sufficient weight to the Spirit. Can we think of the Spirit as having identity outside the "space" between the Father and the Son, but still in relationship with them? Such a question reflects the delight of continuing to learn more about the depths of God's own life.

Finally, the divinity of the Holy Spirit may also come into the thinking of feminist theologians. Some feminist theologians have suggested that the Holy Spirit represents the feminine in God's life and identity. That suggestion has not received widespread acceptance in any school of theology. Many theologians reject it because it wrongly introduces the notion of sex and gender into God. Even those who may be open to such a notion recognize that regarding the Spirit as the feminine in the life and work of God, by locating the feminine in a doctrine that has been traditionally neglected, has the strong tendency to perpetuate the very attitudes that feminist theology seeks to overcome.

The Holy Spirit and Jesus Christ

The doctrine of the Holy Spirit is well developed in relation to Jesus Christ. Some theologies draw on emphases that are relatively clear in Scripture, in which Jesus is the bearer of the Spirit and the sender of the Spirit. These two emphases are often regarded as representing the approaches of the synoptic Gospels (Jesus the bearer of the Spirit) and the Gospel of John (Jesus the sender of the Spirit).

Another development in the doctrine of the Holy Spirit is represented in some theologies that argue for a "Spirit Christology." This doctrinal emphasis usually points out that the story of Jesus Christ can easily be seen as focused on the work of the Spirit. The Spirit is the agent of conception and shapes the preparation for the birth. The early prophecies that greet Jesus' birth are also the work of the Spirit. It is the Spirit who drives Jesus into the desert and empowers his ministry. And it is this Spirit who, at least in some NT passages, is the power of resurrection.

Most theologies still teach the traditional ordering of Jesus' ministry and mission as the foundation for the work of the Spirit, whose work is the continuation of Jesus' ministry and mission. But some theologies change this ordering slightly to give greater consideration to the mission of the Holy Spirit from the very beginning of the story of Jesus Christ. Indeed, if we see the gospel as the story of salvation, then we may be able to consider more ways, such as this one, to vary our emphasis in telling the story and thus more ways of teaching the doctrine that guides and guards the story as we live it and tell it.

The Holy Spirit and Creation

In the chapter on the doctrine of creation, I note the relative neglect of that doctrine in theology. When we bring together that neglect and the neglect of the doctrine of the Holy Spirit, we are in an area of theology that is often very thin, sometimes even nonexistent. Some theologies may note the presence of God's "Spirit" in the Genesis narrative (1:2). Is this the Spirit, the third person of the Trinity, or is this the "spirit" that is a more general reference to God's presence? Similarly, some theologies may note the work of the Spirit in sustaining the life of creation (as in Ps. 103) and anticipating the redemption of creation (Rom. 8). But such discussion is still relatively rare. Some recent developments toward a more trinitarian doctrine of creation should also lead to more attention to the role of the Spirit in creation. Among theologians who are already thinking along these lines, the work of the Spirit in creation offers new ways to address questions of evolution in the light of the continuing work of the Spirit in creation. Some theologians have also found doctrinal guidance for environmental concerns in light of the Spirit's work in sustaining created life.

The Holy Spirit and Salvation

In the work of salvation, the doctrine of the Holy Spirit clearly occupies center stage as the Spirit applies what Christ accomplishes. In the chapter on salvation I point out that many theologies broaden the scope of salvation beyond a concern merely for individuals to include the cosmos. The work of the Spirit in the salvation of the cosmos from the power of evil is an important one that a few theologies are addressing. But in most theologies, the work of the Spirit in salvation concerns human beings.

In the work of the salvation of humankind, the Spirit may be thought of as the one who converts, matures, and equips. Not all these aspects of salvation will be found in every theology, nor will the work of the Spirit always be regarded in the same way.

The converting work of the Spirit may be described by a variety of terms. Which terms are used may reflect an emphasis on one aspect or understanding of conversion. Does the Spirit bring us to faith? Make us "born again"? Make us "new"? Bring us into God's family? And so on. None of these descriptions captures by itself the full meaning of the work of salvation. Even my use of the term "conversion" reflects a particular approach to the work of the Holy Spirit in salvation. All of these terms are biblical, so the question to ponder is how the work of the Holy Spirit is taught through the use of them. In particular, we may learn a lot by noting which term receives the most emphasis in a theology and how that choice shapes an understanding of the Holy Spirit.

The doctrine of the Holy Spirit may engage a number of other aspects of the doctrine of salvation. Several are treated in the chapter on salvation, among them questions of predestination, election, grace, and perseverance. But one question that fits more readily here is the work of the Holy Spirit in maturing believers by making them holy. This is the work of sanctification in the lives of those who have already come to faith in Jesus Christ. In the Christian tradition, all strands agree that one work of the Holy Spirit is this work of making us holy. But there is disagreement over how this work takes place. Not all theologies will give attention to this question, but those that do may take several different approaches.

Many theologies will seek the Spirit's work of sanctification as a progressive work requiring lots of discipline and struggle, typically accompanied by setbacks and successes. Overall this process moves toward increasing holiness, but it is never complete in this life. As a general rule this view is taught by theologies in the Reformed and Lutheran traditions, including those strands strongly influenced by them, such as Baptists.

In contrast to this view, some theologies teach that while we may progress toward holiness for a time, there is also the promise, the hope, the expectation that at some point the Holy Spirit will work in an instant to make us holy. This instantaneous work of the Spirit is usually regarded as the moment when we are made entirely holy. Thus, it is sometimes called "entire sanctification" or "perfection." This view draws on the teaching of John Wesley, who did not claim such holiness for himself or regard it as the possession of most believers. The churches that descend from Wesley disagree among themselves on this teaching. Some, such as Nazarenes and Wesleyans, have historically made it an important part of their teaching. The United Methodists, on the other hand, do not teach the doctrine. It is also the case that theologians in these traditions differ on the meaning of "entire sanctification."

Finally, I should note an entirely different approach to the work the Holy Spirit in "salvation" that is taken by the Anabaptist tradition. For this movement, which arose at the time of the Reformation and continues today in the Mennonite church and similar groups, emphasis should be placed not on the work of the Spirit in "salvation," but on the Spirit's work in making us disciples of Jesus Christ. For them our concern should not be on getting saved or being saved but on following Jesus. The work of the Spirit is to empower us for that path of discipleship.

Thus far I have identified the Holy Spirit and salvation in relation to the Spirit's converting and maturing work. The third work of the Spirit, equipping, takes us into the doctrine of the church.

The Holy Spirit and the Church

The great tradition of the church agrees that the church is called into being by the Holy Spirit on the basis of Christ's work in fulfilling the will of the Father. The tradition also agrees that the church owes its character to the Holy Spirit. These agreements are discussed at length in the chapter on the church.

Within this broad and significant agreement, there are some differences on the work of the Holy Spirit in the church. The most significant concerns the work of the Spirit to equip the church for its ministry and mission. Various emphases and concerns may be found in this area. One of the most significant historically has been the teaching of churches in the Pentecostal and charismatic traditions. These two traditions sometimes vary a bit on their teachings, but in their agreement they stand in contrast to other traditions.

The point of difference concerns the teaching of the church on certain gifts of the Spirit that are often labeled "miraculous" or "sign" gifts. These gifts include working miracles, prophesying, speaking in tongues, and interpreting tongues (see 1 Cor. 12–14). Often, tongues speaking is the specific focus. This gift of the Spirit is central to the teaching and identity of Pentecostal churches. It may be slightly less significant in charismatic churches, but these labels are quite fluid and in themselves tell us very little.

Historically, the Pentecostal churches look back to the day of Pentecost described in Acts 2, but they more recently trace their origins to the early twentieth century. At that time Pentecostals argued for the continuing gift of tongues today and its practice as the sign of "baptism in the Holy Spirit" that empowers believers for service. This teaching stood over against the teaching of most churches at that time that the miraculous gifts, including tongues, are no longer given by the Spirit. Today the contrast is less sharp. Many churches outside the Pentecostal tradition may accept the availability of tongues but differ over its significance and the "baptism of the Holy Spirit."

Beyond this difference, the work of the Holy Spirit to equip the church for ministry and mission is an important theme in many theologies. Among various church traditions, the gifts of the Spirit are regarded as crucial to the health of the church and its life. How those gifts are distributed among the people of God in the church remains a point of debate. But what is not in question is the necessity of the power of the Holy Spirit for the life of the church.

The Holy Spirit and the Bible

One of the ways that the power of the Holy Spirit works in the church is through the Bible. In Chapter 1, the role of the Bible relates to the task of theology at several points. As I note there, the role and authority of the Bible for theology varies among theologians and schools of theology. When we bring the Holy Spirit into focus, one significant area of doctrine is the connection between the Spirit and the Bible. This work is so significant that many theologies devote an entire chapter to the Bible separate from any other doctrine. But even in those theologies, the central question is still the work of the Spirit.

The relationship between the Holy Spirit and the Bible may be neatly divided into three parts for the purpose of doctrinal clarity: the initial recognition of God and God's work, the writing down of an account of God's identity and activity, and the reception of that written account by its readers and hearers. Although we can distinguish these elements for the purpose of analysis and reflection, in practice we cannot separate them so neatly.

The accounts that are written in the Bible begin with the recognition that God is revealing God's identity and God's activity through a whole variety of means: acting, speaking, giving dreams, and many more ways that all reach fulfillment in Jesus Christ. For some, these accounts are merely human records of religious experience that have weight for us because they are a part of the history of our community. But for other theologians, the recognition of God depends upon the work of the Holy Spirit opening eyes and ears to receive God's revelation. These latter theologians may differ in their account of how the Spirit accomplishes this purpose, but they agree that humankind would not recognize and receive God's revelation apart from the work of the Spirit.

For theologians who see the work of the Spirit in this recognition and reception of God's revelation, the next consideration is the work of the Holy Spirit as God's revelation is written down and becomes the Bible. This is one of the thorniest issues in Christian doctrine: How does the Holy Spirit work in the writing of the Bible? Clearly the Bible is the product of human activity. But just as clearly both the OT and the NT claim that God is at work in their being written. How do these two, the human authors and the Holy Spirit, work together? Does the influence of one override the other? Do the limitations of the human authors restrict the work of the Spirit? If the Spirit is not bound by the limitations of human authors, does the power of the Spirit eradicate the human contribution? These are the kinds of issues that theologians may wrestle with.

This initial question concerns the influence of the Holy Spirit on the human authors of the Bible. But that question soon develops further into a question about the Bible that comes to be written. On this question, theologians may engage in lively debates over the nature of the Bible. Terms like "infallibility" and "inerrancy" are defined and debated. Not all theologians enter this far into the relationship between the Holy Spirit and the Bible.

Some are content to say that the Holy Spirit works in the writing of the Bible so that the Bible is trustworthy and authoritative, without needing to be more specific about the work of the Spirit.

For many theologians, the relationship between the Holy Spirit and the Bible is not complete until the Bible becomes the means by which we come to know the good news of Jesus Christ, believe in him, become members of Christ and his church, and follow the way that he teaches. In other words, the Holy Spirit works through the Bible and in us to bring us into the life of faith in Jesus Christ. This work of the Spirit is closely tied to the doctrine of salvation, but in some theologies it may also have a special focus on the way that the work of the Spirit is tied to the Bible.

Finally, we may note that some theologies would include in the account that I have just given a greater emphasis on the community through which the Holy Spirit works. We have a tendency today to think of individuals recognizing God's work, writing the Bible, and receiving its teaching. But in the Bible itself, according to some theologians, the community is more important than the individual. It is the community that discerns God's revelation. Although an individual must perform the physical act of writing, it is the community that has developed the laws, received the poetry, formed the wisdom, discerned true prophecy and preserved it, told and retold the Gospels, and shaped the NT letters. This emphasis on community may also lead theologians to some consideration of the formation of the biblical canon, an area often neglected by theologians. In this approach it is also the community today that works together under the guidance of the Holy Spirit to hear the continuing teaching and authority of the Bible.

Conclusion

The content of this chapter overlaps significantly with that of other chapters. This repetition should be helpful in grasping the interweaving of Christian doctrines and in beginning the work of

Conclusion

grappling with their depths. The topics covered in this chapter are some of the most significant for the doctrine of the Holy Spirit, but they are not the only ones that may be treated as part of that doctrine. Indeed, as I have indicated, we may be near the beginning of a fresh appreciation and account of the Holy Spirit that will generate further understanding of the good news of Jesus Christ and greater faithfulness in our witness to him.

CHAPTER 6

Creation

The doctrine of creation is the study of the cosmos — all that exists — as a result of God's activity. In many settings today the first thing that comes to mind when "creation" is mentioned is evolution. In fact, this controversy has become so dominant in our culture that we have trouble thinking that creation is concerned with anything else. Sometimes works of Christian theology can reinforce that habit of connecting the doctrine of creation with the controversy over evolution. Theologies do that by downplaying the importance of the doctrine or by surrendering it to "science" — as if any talk of God as creator is embarrassing in today's culture.

Theologies often downplay the doctrine by placing it under another doctrine or by providing a brief discussion of creation relative to other doctrines. In such cases "creation" may become merely an account of humankind, or it may be briefly discussed under the doctrine of God. Other theologies provide no real doctrine of creation but instead present some "results of science" as the truthful account of the cosmos.

Each of these instances is a symptom of the recent history of theology in relation to the various sciences. For over two hundred years theology has had a tendency to surrender talk about the cosmos to the sciences. There are some exceptions to this, as I will note below, but the dominant theological tendency has been to recognize (capitulate to?) the power and privilege of science in western European society. As a result, many theologies have retreated from claims about the cosmos and have been content to make claims only about human experience — social and individual.

In the last part of the twentieth century and the early years of the twenty-first century, the relationship between science and religion is a renewed topic of conversation. In North America, that conversation has focused significantly not just on "science and religion" but even more closely on the relationship between Christian theology and science. This discussion is a complex one that raises many questions. For the purposes of this primer, we must note that the relative lack of development in the Christian doctrine of creation over the last two centuries may mean that the discussion of these relationships is premature unless it first stimulates more consideration of the doctrine of creation.

But the landscape of Christian theology is not entirely bleak when one looks for the doctrine of creation. In those theologies that provide relatively significant discussions of the doctrine, we find a number of issues. Although other theologies may organize these issues in various ways and consider some but not all of them, I will introduce you to the doctrine by considering the origin, continuation, scope, and end (or goal) of creation. But first we must consider the role of the Bible.

The Role of the Bible

More than any other doctrine, the doctrine of creation seems to bring into focus issues concerning the cultural particularity, the literary forms, and the authority of the Bible. Decisions on these issues may be determinative for the development of a doctrine of creation. At the same time, the relationships among these issues are complex, so you may find theologians representing a wide range of positions on them.

The issue of cultural particularity comes into play when we

recognize that the biblical texts were written before the rise of contemporary science — they were produced by particular cultures very different from our own culture. Does this mean that they are so dated — so bound to previous cultures — that they are of no use to us today in developing a doctrine of creation? In other words, are our concerns with creation today so different from those of biblical times that the Bible has no relevance for us? Or are the texts, though shaped by the cultures that produced them, still valuable for developing a doctrine of creation? Is this doctrine a concern that persists through time and culture, so that the Bible still provides guidance today? Indeed, some theologians go further, arguing that the Bible, not science, sets the agenda for the doctrine of creation. The question for these theologians is not whether the Bible is still relevant in an age of science, but whether science addresses the really significant issues with which the Bible is concerned.

Theologians who conclude that the cultural particularity of the biblical texts renders them useless today may not even consider further questions about the biblical text. But for many, the issue of cultural particularity is intertwined with the issue of the literary form (sometimes called "genre") of the biblical texts on creation. Anyone who has ever read a daily newspaper has dealt with the necessity of reading different literary forms in different ways. We read "differently" depending on whether we are reading comic strips, editorials, news reports, movie reviews, stock market quotations, and so on. Here is the issue for each biblical text on creation: What is its literary form, its genre? Is it scientific literature? A historical account? A liturgical text? A poetic celebration? Saga, myth, parable, torah? How this question is answered usually has a significant effect on a particular account of the doctrine of creation. If a biblical text is judged to be scientific literature, then a theologian has to deal in specific ways with the conflict between the biblical text and scientific accounts. If a biblical text on creation is judged to be a liturgical text, then a theologian may have a different set of conflicts to consider.

The questions here are complex. They involve questions

about the source(s) of authority for theology, the practice of biblical interpretation, and the role of culture in shaping our thoughts and lives. Theologians wrestle with these issues implicitly and explicitly in their works. Nowhere are the issues more complex than with the doctrine of creation. In the end, the issue is whether the biblical texts have authority in the development of a doctrine of creation, and if so, how that authority functions.

For example, theologians who regard the Bible as bound to prescientific culture, that is, culture prior to the rise of modern science, will give little if any attention to the Bible in developing a doctrine of creation. For them the doctrine must be developed on other bases — such as the natural sciences. For others the doctrine is developed through a mutually correcting and illuminating dialogue between the Bible and science. For some the Bible's account of creation simply gives a different perspective that neither conflicts with nor corrects science. For still others, the Bible yields an authoritative account of creation that conflicts in significant ways with contemporary science.

Yes, but only in a very small percentage

Of course, my description of these approaches is too general to be entirely fair to any theologian. And many theologians will adopt different positions depending upon the biblical text or scientific issue under consideration. But these descriptions will give you a place to start in your study of the doctrine of creation.

The Origin of Creation

When we think about creation today, many of us have in mind a specific act — the act of creation — that brought the cosmos into existence. When we think in this way, we are thinking of creation as an act that is complete. In Christian doctrine this way of thinking may be discussed as "the origin of creation." But even here the discussion is usually more nuanced than our casual ways of thinking and speaking. For Christian doctrine "creation" is not just about a onetime, completed act. Even when we think about the origin of creation, we do not reduce the doctrine merely to this issue. As we will see below, the doctrine of creation concerns more than the origin of creation.

Nevertheless, it is concerned with the "origin" of creation. For most, "origin" has to do with the beginning of creation. A Latin phrase *creatio ex nihilo* ("creation from nothing"), is often used to affirm that the cosmos has an absolute beginning point in the activity of God. This affirmation brings the doctrine into direct relationship with contemporary scientific claims. At times science has denied the possibility (for example, arguing for an "infinitely expanding universe"), at other times science has supported it (for example, with the big bang theory).

Quite apart from science, some theologians have argued for an "origin" of creation that is not an absolute beginning. Most of us, who are used to reading "in the beginning" as the first words of the Bible, may have difficulty with the idea that "origin" could mean something other than absolute beginning. However, some have argued that a better translation of the first verse of the Bible is "when God began to create. . . ." So some theologians argue that the Bible really isn't concerned with origin as absolute beginning, but with origin more in the sense of "foundation." These theologians may argue that the Bible just doesn't speculate about the origin of the cosmos, but does strongly affirm the dependence of the cosmos upon God for its existence without asking or answering questions about when and how an act of creation took place.

The Continuation of Creation

Although the origin of creation may be dominant in a lot of casual thinking about the doctrine, the continuation of creation also plays a role in more formal reflection on the doctrine. If we are only concerned with God as creator in a onetime, completed act of creation, then we are neglecting God's continuing relationship to the cosmos. If we go too far with this neglect, we may end up with a view that has been labeled "deism." Deism stands for a family of views that have in common the belief that after the onetime act of creation, God ceased to have any relationship to the world. On this view there is a moral structure built into the universe and human nature. Human beings have immortal souls whose existence continues beyond physical death. But God does not continue to interact with creation. This view seeks to free theology from the challenges of science and denies all the traditional Christian claims about Jesus Christ.

Christian theology has strongly rejected deism and views that seem to be approaching it. But at the same time, theologians have disagreed on how to describe God's continuing work of creation. They want to avoid simply identifying God with the cosmos (a view called pantheism). So how do we walk this fine line between separating God too much from the cosmos (the mistake of deism) and identifying God too closely with the cosmos (the mistake of pantheism)?

To answer that question, some today have proposed a view they label panentheism. These theologians have argued in various ways that God is continuously and intimately involved with the cosmos but is not to be identified with it. This view ties God's life closely to the cosmos but does not reduce it to the life of the cosmos as pantheism does. Some panentheists tie their view to a particular account of God as triune creator. This view has generated considerable discussion and caused considerable controversy.

Another answer draws on the doctrine of God as triune in ways significantly different from panentheism. These trinitarian theologians argue that God's continuing work as creator is triune in shape. That is, each "person" of the Trinity has a particular relationship to the cosmos. Thus, for example, while the Holy Spirit may have a continuous, intimate relationship with the cosmos, the Father has a different relationship to the cosmos, as does the Son. In this way both the "nearness" and "distance" of God may be affirmed.

Here, as in many other places, theologians' careful reflection goes beyond our often casual ways of thinking about God and the cosmos. Many complex issues surround the continuing relationship between God and the cosmos. Theologians offer us various ways of resolving those issues. While we may never reach consensus on an answer, we may learn from the debate to work hard at maintaining that balance between nearness and distance.

The Scope of Creation

In one sense we have already been considering the scope of creation as we think beyond questions of origin to consider also the question of continuation. But there is another way to think about scope as well, and that is to reflect on what theologians include in their discussion of the doctrine of creation. Here I mean not so much the *activities* that may be involved in creation, but the *things* that may be studied under the doctrine of creation.

I noted above that some theologians tend to reduce "creation" to the study of humankind. In those theologies there may be a brief discussion of creation under the doctrine of God, where God may be studied as creator, but additional discussion would be limited to a separate chapter on humankind.

Other theologies, however, may go further in the "things" they consider under the doctrine of creation. These theologians may, for example, consider the status of nonhuman life as God's creation. Does Christian theology teach us anything about plants and animals that is special to Christianity? Some theologians may even extend our thinking beyond forms of life to consider the value of other parts of creation, such as stars and planets.

Beyond these things that we may think of as part of the natural order, some theologians also ask us to consider such things as culture and unseen spiritual forces. If culture is what we humans do with the stuff of creation, then it may be appropriately studied as part of the doctrine of creation. Here the doctrine may study social, political, economic, and other manifestations of culture. For some theologians this study may go beyond what is seen to what is unseen, in the study of spiritual forces that may be manifested in a variety of ways. The relationship between these seen and unseen forces is a matter of debate among theologians and does not appear always in a doctrine of creation. But for some theologians these things are important elements of a doctrine of creation.

The End of Creation

When you read the words "end of creation," you probably think of "end" as cessation, as the extinguishing of creation. If it has an absolute beginning, then it has an absolute end, after which creation will no longer exist. But when theologians use the phrase "end of creation," they mean "end" as purpose or goal. To understand this better, think of the end for which one kind of hammer is created — to drive nails and perhaps pull them. Another kind of hammer may be created to pound out dents in an automobile fender. Thinking of end in this way, theologians often consider the "end of creation," or perhaps better, the end for which the cosmos was created.

Indeed, for some theologians the answer to this question is the most important part of the doctrine of creation. Their convictions about God's activity in the origin and continuation of creation are significantly shaped by their convictions about the end of creation. Furthermore, many of these theologians point out that the teaching of the Bible is focused not on the destruction of the cosmos but on the redemption of the cosmos, so that it is a "new creation."

Considering the end of creation leads us to ask, "Where is the cosmos headed?" not "Where did the cosmos begin?"

The Providence of God

The providence of God as God's rule over creation may often be considered as a part of the doctrine of creation. However, it may also be found under the doctrine of God or in a separate treatment. Moreover, answers given here are significantly intertwined with other doctrines such as the doctrine of salvation.

When theologians reflect on the providence of God, they are led to consider the reality of God's rule over the cosmos, the range of God's rule, and the character of that rule, all in relation to the existence of evil. These issues are so tightly related that we will consider them together, rather than trying artificially to separate them.

Perhaps the best way to prepare for theological study on these issues is to recognize the range of questions that may be asked. Does God rule over the cosmos? If not, then in what sense is "God" actually "God"? If God does rule over the cosmos, does God rule over all of the cosmos? Does God control not only the overall continuing existence of the cosmos and its destiny, but also the tiny happenings of the cosmos? Does God rule over planetary orbits? The course of my life? The bug that just landed on my computer screen? And how do we understand God's rule over a world marked by evil? Does God "rule" over a world marked by deadly viruses, genocide, sexual abuse, murder, lying, and so on?

Theologians approach these questions from many different directions. Some look primarily to the Bible and seek to show how our lives and history must be interpreted in the light of its teaching. Others begin with our experience and seek to understand how the claims of the Bible can be true given our knowledge and experience of evil in the world. Some draw significantly on philosophical reflection; others focus on the significance of God becoming human in Jesus Christ and suffering as we suffer. Others focus on the final conquest of evil at the "end" of creation. And many weave together several of these approaches.

Some theologies attempt to explain the existence of evil so that it makes sense. Other theologians regard that attempt as doomed to failure — since evil is something that has gone wrong in the cosmos, any attempt to make it seem right is bound to fail. For these theologians, Christians may be able to show that we are not acting foolishly or irrationally when we confess belief in

76

God in a world marked by evil. But we cannot explain why evil exists in order to make sense of it, because evil by definition is senseless.

One other issue regarding evil has to be considered under the doctrine of creation — the origin of evil. We often, in our casual thinking, regard evil as a "thing," something that exists. But if evil is a thing, where did it come from? Did God create it? If so, then how can we say that God is entirely good and does no evil? If God did not create evil, is there another being in the cosmos capable of creating? If so, then God is not the only creator. These kinds of difficulties have led Christian theologians to recognize that evil is not a thing. That is, it has no independent existence of its own. Evil only exists as a distortion of or defect in the good things that God has created. This conviction is presented in different ways by various theologians and is not accepted by all. But it has been and still is the dominant understanding of the origin of evil: Everything in the cosmos is created as good by God and is by nature good. Evil is the distortion of the good that God creates. This conviction is not only the result of the kind of thinking that I noted above. It is also the basis or consequence of the Christian conviction that the cosmos is redeemable.

Conclusion

The doctrine of creation may or may not receive significant treatment in a particular theology. Sometimes the elements of the doctrine are scattered throughout a theological work. In an age of science such as ours, the doctrine of creation is vitally important. At the same time, it may also be very difficult to develop a doctrine of creation when so few theologians have devoted significant reflection to it and when the dominance of science suppresses theological reflection on creation.

CHAPTER 7

Humankind

What do we know better than ourselves? But do we really know ourselves? When we study the Christian doctrine of humankind, we seek to think theologically about ourselves. In some theologies this doctrine is called the study of man or mankind. In the past, "man" and "mankind" were used to include the entire human race, male and female. Today, however, many people have judged that such language is understood exclusively, as referring only to males. Some also argue that even in the past, this language tended to place a primary emphasis on males. We will consider this issue later; for now I want simply to note that my use of "humankind" is a recognition of this concern with language and doctrine.

The doctrine of humankind may be called anthropology (from the Greek *anthropos*). This can be confusing, because we also have today a social science called anthropology. Therefore, the Christian doctrine of humankind is sometimes called theological anthropology. This doctrine brings theology into relationships with other disciplines like anthropology, psychology, history, biology, and philosophy. All of these also study humankind in various ways. Similarly, the doctrine of humankind brings us into close contact with our own experience.

For these reasons, decisions about sources and authority for theology become particularly clear at this point. Some theologians rely entirely or almost entirely on the Bible and Christian tradition to develop their doctrine of humankind. If they refer to our experience or other disciplines, they do so to judge their adequacy in relation to Christian doctrine. Other theologians may weave together the Bible, tradition, experience, and other sources. Some of them argue that because God is creator, we can know something, perhaps a lot, about humankind by studying creation today. These theologians think we can develop a "natural theology" — a theology derived from studying the order of nature — but they typically subordinate that natural theology to biblical theology. And they argue that although we can know something from nature, the central truths of Christianity, including God's work of redemption, can only be known through God's revelation in Scripture. Still other theologians grant primary authority to our experience and other disciplines. They admit the teaching of the Bible and tradition only where they agree with contemporary sources. For them the Bible is not God's revelation, but simply a record of human reflection that is a mixture of truth and error.

The decisions theologians make here are difficult to identify and describe. You need to know two things. First, theologians do make important decisions about sources and authority as they develop the doctrine of humankind. These decisions are made everywhere in Christian doctrine, but they are particularly evident with this doctrine because it is about our experience and because so many other disciplines also make claims about humankind. Secondly, using something as a source is not the same as granting it authority. Sometimes theologians draw on human experience or some scholarly discipline to show how mistaken we can be when our beliefs are judged by the Bible and Christian tradition. At other times they draw on the Bible to show how our experience or some discipline corrects those earlier, "culture-bound" beliefs. To complicate matters further, sometimes a theologian may seek to correct an earlier, mistaken interpretation of the Bible in order to establish a "better" interpretation. This theologian is attacking mistaken interpretations of the Bible, not the authority of the Bible. Indeed, because she believes in biblical authority, she may be particularly concerned to identify mistaken interpretations.

When theologians draw on sources other than the Bible and Christian tradition, the situation becomes even more complex. When they draw on human experience as a source for theology, they must contend with different interpretations of experience. "Experience" is never just an experience; it is always interpreted experience. And interpretations of experience differ. Likewise, when theologians draw on other disciplines, they must consider the differences within those disciplines. Anthropologists, psychologists, historians, biologists, and philosophers disagree among themselves on many issues.

Before we consider specific topics, I must note one other general theme that pervades any doctrine of humankind. As theologians develop a theological anthropology, one of the decisions they must make is the relative weight to give to humankind as created, humankind as fallen, humankind as redeemed, and humankind as glorified beyond death. These decisions will depend on the judgment a theologian makes about how much we can know of each of these and about which is most important.

In this chapter I will introduce you to the main issues addressed by theological anthropologies. Some of the differences among theologians are fundamental and result in very different, incompatible doctrines. Others are more a matter of structure and emphasis; here the doctrine may be different but the accounts compatible with one another. As we explore the Christian doctrine of humankind, then, we will keep in mind the limits of human knowledge even of ourselves. And we will seek to know ourselves in light of God's knowledge of us.

Three Issues

Before we consider some of the specific themes found in the Christian doctrine of humankind, we will examine three basic issues. These issues are not addressed by every theologian, but they do shape various presentations of theological anthropology. All theologians make explicit or implicit judgments on these issues as they develop a doctrine of humankind.

Human Nature

Most of us are used to thinking in terms of human nature. Indeed, you may have thought that "human nature" is a good description of the subject matter of this chapter. Moreover, much of the Christian tradition uses the term "human nature" for the doctrine of humankind. Today, however, not everyone thinks "human nature" is an appropriate term.

Theologians who use this terminology to develop Christian doctrine teach that every human being has a "nature" that identifies that human being and unites all of us as human. They may develop their account of human nature from the Bible, but they would argue that every human being in every time and place has that same nature. Whatever your profession, your social location, your race, or your sex, you have the same nature. That nature makes you human. It does not change over time or place. It is the essence of what makes us human.

Some theologians today, in concert with some anthropologists, sociologists, and others, are questioning this notion of human nature. Can we really say that a stockbroker in New York and a herdsman in Kenya have the same nature that makes them human? Isn't the cultural shape of our humanity so significant that we have to say there is no essence that makes us human? These theologians are particularly concerned that our concept of human nature has been shaped almost entirely by western European history. If he had the opportunity, wouldn't an African villager give an account of humankind very different from the Western account of human nature? In fact, what we often find in other cultures is not an account of humankind as a whole, but an account of their own group or "tribe" (which itself is a Western term not found among those we call "tribes").

81

Confronted with this reality and its challenge, some theologians are rethinking the Christian doctrine of humankind. Some find in the biblical teaching a response to this challenge that asserts the unity of the human race as created by God, as sinners separated from God, and as those loved by God in Jesus Christ. On this basis they continue to assert a doctrine of human nature. Other theologians find the term and the idea problematic and seek other ways to give an account of humankind.

Human Relationships

Some theologians develop a doctrine of humankind by emphasizing the relationships with which we live. Some of these theologians may also give an account of human nature or argue that the relationships are the essence of what it means to be human. For these theologians it is not just the relationships that make us human, but also the nature of those relationships.

These theologians will identify a variety of relationships. The most basic is our relationship to God. Of course, all creation has a relationship to God. It is the particular shape of our relationship to God that makes us human and not a dog or a rock. Similarly, we have a relationship to the rest of creation that makes us human because of its particular shape. We also have a special relationship to other humans that nothing else in creation has. Finally, some of these theologians will also include our relationship to ourselves. Human beings, they argue, are self-conscious in a way that no other part of creation is.

This relationality is an important element in many contemporary theologies. Sometimes it is presented as a description of human nature, sometimes as complementary to an account of human nature, and sometimes as an alternative. In every case, accounts of humankind as relational tend to move away from the static, timeless account of humankind that we find typically in theological anthropologies that emphasize human nature.

Humankind and Culture

Moving still further away from accounts of humankind as possessing a timeless human nature, some theologians locate humankind within particular cultures. These accounts are often the constructive doctrine of those theologians noted above who criticize accounts of human nature.

Theologians who develop a doctrine of humankind in relation to culture want to historicize their doctrine. That is, they always want to locate doctrine in relation to a particular time and place. For them there is no essence of humankind that pervades all times and places. Rather, each time and place produces its own doctrine of humankind. What it meant to be human in European feudal society is different from what it means in the capitalist society of twenty-first-century North America. These theologians emphasize the construction of meaning by culture. What we mean by "humankind" varies from culture to culture.

Some theologians may accept this assertion as an observation of the way cultures work but then criticize those cultural constructions in the light of biblical teaching and Christian tradition. For example, they may agree that capitalism creates a particular understanding of what it means to be human, but then declare that understanding wrong in the light of biblical teaching. Other theologians see cultural constructions of what it means to be human as setting the limits for Christian doctrine. Here doctrine is adjusted to fit a particular time and place. The Bible does not exercise primary authority because it reflects the cultural constructions of another time and place.

Image of God

In the Bible and in the Christian tradition, one of the dominant categories for the doctrine of humankind is "the image of God," or in a Latin phrase, the *imago Dei.* Although this phrase occurs only a few times in the Bible, its use at the creation of humankind (Gen. 1:26-27) makes it foundational. Theologians who use the phrase develop it in relation to other judgments they make about humankind. Sometimes they develop the image of God as a reference to human nature. In the tradition, theologians have identified a variety of specific human characteristics as this image of God — that we are to rule over creation, that we are persons, that we have rationality, that we are self-conscious, and others. At other times they develop the image of God as a reference to our relationality. They then give the kinds of accounts that I noted above. Other theologians make very little if any use of the image of God in their theological anthropology. For them the Bible gives us little guidance as to the meaning of "image of God," and the phrase has no significance in our own culture.

Human Sexuality

One of the areas of greatest controversy today concerns the Christian doctrine of human sexuality. This controversy intertwines with questions about human nature, relationships, and cultural constructions of human nature. One issue where these questions come into focus is the relationship of men and women. I will briefly introduce the substance of this controversy, then describe the way the arguments are conducted. The controversy over Christian teaching on the relationship between men and women concerns three issues: how men and women are to relate to one another generally, how husbands and wives are to relate, and the ordination of women as priests or pastors.

The first issue concerns the social status of men and women according to Christian doctrine. What should we say and do about a world where women are paid less than men for the same job? Where women are much more likely to be the victims of abuse? Where women have fewer legal and social protections than men? Does the Bible condone such circumstances and structures? Does the Bible teach the subordination of women but call us to justice? Does the Bible call for the liberation of women and the equality of men and women?

In response to such questions some theologians assert that the Bible does indeed teach the subordination of women to men. The injustice and oppression that we see in the world is the result of sin. Christians should work to overcome the oppression and injustice of sin. But even when we overturn the effects of sin, women will still be subordinate to men. Other theologians argue that the Bible describes a patriarchal society that subordinates women to men, but that within that account it also calls us to something more. For these theologians the subordination of women to men is itself a product of sin. When Christians work to overcome sin, we should work to erase this subordination and establish a society where men and women are equal in Christ. Still other theologians regard the Bible as intrinsically patriarchal and sexist. For them the Bible itself and not just the society it describes must be overcome if we are to establish justice and equality for all. Some of these theologians may argue that the Bible calls Christians to work for liberation and justice. These see the Bible as giving Christians general directions for our work, but the culture it reflects and the specific teachings it contains regarding men and women must be set aside if we are to be faithful to its central concern for justice and liberation.

The issue of the relationship between husbands and wives reflects many of the same debates and positions that we just considered. I will note one complication that may arise in some theologians. There are a number of conservative theologians who argue that the Bible calls for liberation and justice for women (and men) in society but teaches the subordination of wives to their husbands. They argue that husbands should love their wives and treat them justly, but they also argue that the husband is the one who rules ("lovingly") over the home. As with the previous issue, some other theologians argue, to the contrary, that the Bible contains teaching that subverts the "rule" of the husband and should result in Christian marriages where husbands and wives are equal, or as some want to say, where husbands and wives are mutually submissive to one another. Still others advocate egalitarian marriage but see no hope of grounding such marriages in biblical teaching.

The issue of the ordination of women has many facets. In some churches ordination means approval to celebrate or oversee the celebration of the sacraments of Eucharist ("communion") and baptism. In other churches ordination means approval to preach or govern the church. The way arguments are formulated for and against women's ordination often depends on the meaning of ordination in a particular setting. Again, the arguments usually turn on how we interpret the Bible and regard its authority. Some theologians argue that the Bible is authoritative and prohibits the ordination of women in all times and places. Others argue that the Bible is authoritative, that it prohibits the ordination of women in some circumstances, but that it allows and even encourages it in other circumstances. Still other theologians argue that the Bible prohibits the ordination of women but that in doing so it reflects the prejudice of its culture that we should set aside today.

"Ordination" is often the way this debate is described, but some theologians also argue that the issue is really about the ministry of women in the church. What areas of ministry are open to women and to whom are they called to minister? Some churches are committed to the ordination of women but provide them with few places to minister and in practice exclude them from preaching or the position of senior pastor. Others ordain women but restrict their ministry to other women and children. These theologians may point out that churches that did not ordain women nevertheless sent them overseas as single missionaries, entrusting them to bring the gospel to people who had never heard it.

The preceding discussion barely scratches the surface of theological discussions of male-female relationships. And it does not even touch on areas of human sexuality that relate to our sexual identity as heterosexual, homosexual, bisexual, and so on. One of the glaring weaknesses of Christian theology has been its relative neglect of the doctrine of creation and within that doctrine of such issues as human embodiment and sexuality. At this point, you may find little discussion of these issues in a theology text. There are exceptions, and theologians are beginning to direct significant attention to these questions.

Conclusion

Two issues that concern our doctrine of humankind are discussed in the chapter on creation. In the midst of what many identify as an environmental crisis, the relationship between humankind and the rest of creation is receiving special attention. And in a culture where the teaching of evolution is prevalent, the Christian doctrine of humankind faces special challenges.

Finally, the Christian doctrine of humankind is incomplete without significant reference to Christology. If, as Christian doctrine teaches, Jesus Christ is fully human, then he is the fullest revelation of what it means to be human. His righteousness and unbroken fellowship with God and his life of sacrificial love display what it is to be fully human. In that light we are not yet fully human. But by God's grace we may be united with Christ by faith so that by that same grace we may one day be made fully human.

CHAPTER 8

Sin

Sin is one of those concepts in Christian theology that may seem quite obvious in its meaning. Doesn't everyone sin? Doesn't everyone therefore have an understanding of sin? Yes, everyone sins and has some concept of sin. But as we will see, our understanding of sin is profoundly shaped by how we relate the doctrine of sin to the Bible, our experience, and the Christian community. Theology does not invent the complexities that we will encounter; rather, good theology exposes the complexities already present in our sin. By so doing, theology enables us to become more mature in our understanding of sin and God's work to redeem us from sin.

As with many other doctrines, the doctrine of sin is intertwined with other doctrines. How we view sin shapes our doctrine of salvation, and vice versa. Likewise, if Christ came to redeem us from sin, then how we view sin will affect our view of Christ's work. And our view of Christ's work will in turn shape our doctrine of sin. Obviously, our doctrine of sin and our doctrine of humankind are deeply intertwined. For this reason the doctrine of sin is often treated in a chapter on humankind or on creation, but it may also be discussed separately. As I introduce the doctrine of sin, you should keep in mind its relationship to other doctrines.

Sin and Experience

Because sin is so much a part of human experience, how we interpret the role of experience in Christian doctrine is especially important. If a theologian regards experience as more authoritative than the Bible, that produces a particular account of the doctrine of sin. Conversely, if the Bible is regarded as more authoritative than our experience, a different doctrine of sin is forthcoming.

Thus, some theologians hold that the Bible and Christian tradition give us a general concept of sin as that which oppresses us and inhibits our full humanity, but regard the identification of particular sins in the Bible as expressing simply what the biblical authors found oppressive and inhibiting. Today, our experience of sin may be different from that of people in biblical times. For example, the authors of the Bible identify the experience of sexual intercourse outside marriage as "sin." Today, however, some argue that the prohibition of that experience is oppressive and inhibiting. In contrast to biblical culture, some theologians argue that in certain situations sexual intercourse outside marriage is not a sin, but is in fact fulfilling of our humanity as sexual creatures.

Other theologians regard the Bible as more authoritative than experience. For them our experience must be interpreted in the light of Scripture. Thus, even though some may interpret the experience of sexual intercourse outside marriage as liberating, the biblical teaching requires that we reinterpret our experience. Some of these theologians may say that the Christian life is extended training in learning to identify sin in ourselves and in the world so that by God's grace we may overcome it.

Sin and Sins

Some theologians make an explicit distinction between Sin (often capitalized and singular) and sins (not capitalized and often

Sin : sins → disease: symptoms

plural); some make an implicit distinction; others do not recognize the distinction. Those who explicitly or implicitly distinguish the two use "sin" to refer to a power or force and "sins" to refer to particular expressions of that power in specific attitudes and acts.

Some theologians find in the NT the concept of sin as a power or force in the language of "the kingdom of darkness" and "the kingdom of Satan." It may also be expressed in language about evil or in Paul's assertions about our being slaves to sin. The notion of sins as particular expressions of the power of sin is found in places where specific acts such as lying and murder are identified or where attitudes such as envy and lust are condemned. Of course, the language of "acts" and "attitudes" is itself limited because all of these are actions and attitudes. How we distinguish these sins (and whether we should) may also be a topic of concern in Christian doctrine.

Sin as Structural and Personal

Within the context of the distinction between sin and sins, some theologians will also address the nature of sin. Is sin societal or personal? Is sin primarily to be located in unjust, oppressive, and fallen structures of the world — such as economic, political, moral structures — or primarily in persons or individuals? How we answer these questions will influence how we think of salvation and the work of the church. Is the mission of the church primarily to change unjust structures, or is it to change the hearts of individuals? Some theologians place their primary emphasis on one of these doctrines of sin; some seek to emphasize both.

It is probably fair to say that in our culture Christians tend to think of sin as primarily individual — as a matter of the "heart." Even the acts of sin that are obvious, such as lying and murder, are symptoms of a deeper, "heart" condition. However, there is also a significant tradition in Christian doctrine that understands sin as societal and structural. This tradition calls us to recognize that poverty, oppression, and injustice are significant sources of sin. Recently, liberation theology has made a strong case for recovering this view of sin as structural by noting the OT prophets' call to justice, continued in the NT by Jesus' ministry.

Sin(s) and Relationships

One of the primary ways of developing a doctrine of sin is by viewing it as a relational concept. In this approach sin(s) may be viewed in relation to the law of God. Here sin is defined as the breaking of God's law. In relationship to God, sin(s) may be regarded as disobedience to God. Or sin(s) may also be viewed as breaking other relationships for which we are created, such as our relationship to one another, to the rest of creation, and to ourselves. Depending on the emphasis and breadth of a relational view of sin(s), theologians may develop different doctrines. If a theologian includes our relationship to creation in the doctrine of sin(s), this could lead to a theological discussion of the environment. Here it may be helpful to think of sin(s) having a vertical and a horizontal dimension. How these dimensions are brought together shapes a doctrine of sin(s).

Original Sin

One of the most important discussions in the history of Christian theology concerns the doctrine of original sin. Here "original sin" refers to the story of Adam and Eve disobeying God. To what extent does that sin affect the rest of humanity? Are we born "sinners"? If so, are we also born guilty? And if the answer is yes to these questions, then how is that sin and guilt passed on to us and what is God's remedy?

The way theologians answer these questions depends in part on their decisions about the authority of the Bible and the history of Christian doctrine. In the fifth century two theologians, Augustine and Pelagius, debated these issues. After some consideration the church sided with Augustine and condemned Pelagius. Because Pelagius was condemned, few of his writings have survived. However, it seems clear that he denied that the effect of Adam's sin was passed on to the rest of humankind. Thus, Pelagius and his followers argued that we are born without sin and guilt.

The church sided with Augustine in this debate because it viewed the Bible to be on his side and because Pelagius's position seemed to deny the necessity of Christ's death for the forgiveness of sin. Here we can see the intertwining of our doctrine of sin with other doctrines. For many who follow Augustine, his argument provided support for his doctrine of predestination, which will be explained more fully in the chapter on salvation. Here I want briefly to note the connections between different doctrines.

According to Augustine, if we are all born in sin and guilt, then we cannot contribute anything to our salvation. Thus, God must predestine who will be saved. Augustine's doctrine of sin and salvation also shapes his understanding of infant baptism. For him baptism was the washing away of our original sin and guilt. Since babies, who cannot commit sin, are still condemned by their inheritance of Adam's sin and guilt, the only way for them to be saved is through the waters of baptism that wash away their inherited sin and guilt.

It is important to note that some theologians hold to original sin and guilt without accepting Augustine's doctrine of predestination and his view of baptism. The relationship between the original sin of Adam and Eve and our own state is a difficult one. In the end, however, Christian doctrine teaches that we are all sinners, whatever the source of that sin. Thus, we are all in need of a Savior; we cannot save ourselves.

Sin as Pride and Misery

In the history of Christian doctrine sin has been presented predominantly as an expression of our pride (Latin, *hubris*). Sin is our attempt to be our own god. In the Garden of Eden the serpent tells the woman, "You will be like God" (Gen. 3:5). This focus on pride is still a significant interpretation of sin in Christian doctrine. However, some theologians add to it an interpretation of sin as "misery." If pride is thinking more of ourselves than we should, misery is thinking less of ourselves than we should. This view of sin may be found in a number of theologians. Recently, feminist theologians, among others, have been particularly influential in developing it. If we bring these two approaches together, we can see sin, at least in part, as thinking wrongly about our place as human beings in relation to God and the world.

Sin and the Problem of Evil

One of the most significant challenges to Christian faith is the existence of evil in the world. This problem has been with Christianity from its beginning, though it has been approached in many different ways. Christians reject two logically simple answers to the existence of evil: (1) that the world was simply evil from the beginning and always will be, and (2) that evil doesn't really exist, that what we call evil will in the end turn out to be good or an illusion.

The first answer doesn't tell us where we get the idea that something is wrong with this world. In other words, it doesn't answer the problem of goodness. If this world has been evil from its beginning, then where do we get our notion of goodness and our longing for it? The second answer doesn't compel assent because it denies the reality of evil that we all know. In contrast to these views, Christian doctrine asserts that the world was created good and one day will once again be good; it also asserts the reality of evil and God's just dealings with evil.

In the meantime, we are left with the problem of the existence of evil. The theological response to this problem is often called "theodicy." The term comes from the Greek words for God *(Theos)* and justice or justification *(dikaios)*. A theodicy is an attempt to justify belief in a good God in the midst of a world where evil is present.

A minority of theologians respond to the "problem of evil" by asserting that God is good but not all-powerful. In the present, God is struggling against evil just as we are. For these theologians, our belief as Christians is that one day God may finally triumph over evil, but in the meantime God wins some battles with evil and loses others. Most theologians, however, do not accept the denial of God's sovereignty that this view entails.

Some theologians seek to give an explanation for evil — why it exists and the purpose that God puts it to. These theologians are often indebted to an early theologian named Irenaeus (ca. 130–ca. 200), and may give different accounts of how God uses evil. One of the most common is that God uses evil to shape our character and to move us to completeness as human beings.

Other theologians do not try to explain God's use of evil, but instead seek simply to justify our belief in a good and all-powerful God in a world marked by evil. A contemporary Christian philosopher, Alvin Plantinga, has developed a sophisticated philosophical account of the "freewill" defense of Christian faith. Plantinga's account may be simplified almost to the point of misrepresentation by saying that he argues that the best possible world that God could have created is one in which there are creatures who love God freely. If these creatures (in our world, human beings) are to love God freely, they must also be free not to love God. Hence, evil was a possibility in this world from the beginning, and was made actual by human choice. Plantinga's argument has received widespread acceptance. Many have found it to be logically quite persuasive. But others have judged it to be philosophically persuasive and theologically "thin."

Some theologians respond to the problem of evil not by giving an account of its purpose or its logic but by giving an account of how Christianity responds to the fact of evil in the world. That is, given the existence of evil, what are we to do about it? Given our longing for goodness, how are we to become good and make our world good? For these theologians, Christian doctrine provides a "practical" response to the existence of evil. Indeed, they argue that Christianity provides the only hope for a world marked by evil. These theologians find the practical Christian answer to the problem of evil in the cross of Jesus Christ. There God took upon Godself the evil of the world. Through the cross and our identification with Christ's cross, we are transformed, the root of evil in our own lives is eradicated. And through the cross of Christ, one day the entire creation will be purged of evil. In the meantime, we are to cooperate with God's Spirit to erase evil in our own lives and in the world around us. The only power to accomplish that is found in the good news of Jesus Christ.

Conclusion

In various ways Christian doctrine wrestles with the origin, nature, and extent of sin. In the midst of our study we should keep in view three truths. For the Christian, sin is not natural to this world — it is an intrusion that God has begun to eradicate and will one day fully eradicate. In the meantime, the gospel of Jesus Christ provides us with an account of God's response to sin and our responsibility for its presence and its removal. Finally, the Christian doctrine of sin, in concert with other doctrines, guides us to the wonderful news that God loves us and all creation, even in our sin, so much that he gave his Son not "to condemn the world, but in order that the world might be saved through him" (John 3:17).

CHAPTER 9

Salvation

The doctrine of salvation generates considerable interest among Christians, because it is the doctrine that is closest to our experience. Indeed, it is so closely tied to our experience that many Christians already have in place a doctrine of salvation by which to make sense of their experience of salvation. For this reason this doctrine may be very difficult for us to study. That is, if I already have a doctrine of salvation worked out to make sense of my experience, then any challenge to *my* doctrine will also feel like a challenge to my experience, even perhaps to my salvation.

This doctrine is also difficult to study because it sometimes marks a significant difference among Christian traditions. In other words, it sometimes marks the boundary between being part of one Christian tradition or another. On the doctrine of the Trinity, for example, Baptists, Lutherans, Methodists, Presbyterians, Catholics, and others may find general agreement despite some disagreement on details. But on the doctrine of salvation, these groups may have difficulty finding agreement beyond the belief that only God can save us and that God does so through Jesus Christ. Of course, Christian traditions other than the ones I note here hold different views of this doctrine as well.

Although these are real difficulties that we face when studying the doctrine of salvation, we must not let them frustrate our study of Christian doctrine. In fact, we should read the situation in a positive way: the Christian doctrine of salvation is so profound, so rich in meaning, that it cannot be fully captured by any one account. While you may find one or another tradition giving the most satisfying and fullest account of this doctrine, I hope you also find other traditions supplementing and enriching your own.

To prepare you for studying the doctrine of salvation, I will introduce you here to the scope, meaning, order, and means of salvation. These categories will not be found in all theologies, but they do allow me to cover the ground that may be covered in various ways in a Christian doctrine of salvation.

The Scope of Salvation

The phrase "scope of salvation" suggests that I might talk here about how many people are going to be saved. Is everyone going to be saved? Are only a few saved? Are many but not all saved? These are important questions, but I will postpone their consideration until the last chapter. Here I am concerned with a different meaning for the "scope of salvation": Is salvation individual, corporate, or cosmic? (This discussion has close connections and even some overlaps with the discussion of the work of Christ in chapter 4, and the one on the doctrine of sin in chapter 7.)

Many of us Christians in North America, because of our culture and the teaching of our churches, are used to thinking of salvation in individualistic terms. In this way of thinking about salvation, we draw in ways of thinking about other doctrines. Jesus is *my* Savior; he died on the cross for *me*. *My* sins separate me from God; *I* need to be forgiven. *I* must come to faith in Christ; *I* must decide. Theologies that emphasize this doctrine of salvation claim a number of biblical passages for support and may draw on some strand in almost every Christian tradition for support. That is, most traditions within Christianity have some place in their histories where an individualistic doctrine of salvation is present even if it is not the dominant strand.

97

In fact, we may be so used to thinking of salvation in this way that it may seem obviously wrong to suggest or consider other ways to think about it. We portray salvation in individualistic terms in much of our language. Many churches teach us to talk about Jesus as "my" Savior. Many of the songs sung in North American churches reflect and reinforce this individualism. Although we sing the songs as a congregation, we sing about "I," "me," and "my." And those who emphasize the salvation of individuals can draw on significant biblical and historical support.

But other theologians challenge us to think about salvation in other ways. These theologians may challenge us to supplement individualistic thinking with other ways of thinking; some may challenge us to subordinate individualism to another way of thinking; and still others may challenge us to replace individualism with another conception of salvation.

One of those other ways of thinking about salvation is corporate. Theologies that develop this concept of "corporate salvation" urge us to think that in salvation God is gathering together a people. For biblical support they direct our attention to the Old Testament, where God called a nation, Israel, to be God's people. And they suggest that the NT portrays God calling together a new people, the church, made up of all the nations of the earth. This calling of a people is what constitutes salvation in the Bible. Along with this argument, these theologians would further argue for corporate salvation by pointing to many biblical passages where Christ's death and sin are described in corporate terms (Rom. 5:8-11; 2 Cor. 5:18-19; Eph. 1:3-14; 1 Pet. 1:3-9). Many of these passages speak of "we" rather than "I." And often the "you" of the NT is a plural "you" in Greek (the language in which the NT was written), though in English we cannot distinguish the singular and plural "you." (Some readers may think of the "y'all" used in the southern United States, but even that word is often used in the singular. I know; I grew up in Nashville.)

Finally, some theologians urge us to think of the scope of salvation in cosmic terms. They argue that when we consider the full range of language used in the NT to describe salvation, we can see clearly that God's salvation in Christ is concerned with more than just human beings. Therefore, it is not enough to think of salvation in individualistic or even corporate terms, we must also think in cosmic terms. For biblical support these theologians turn to such passages as Colossians 2:20 and to the promise of a new heaven and a new earth — a new creation — in Revelation 21:1-4. This cosmic view challenges us to a more profound vision of the work of Christ and of the nature of sin.

Each of these views claims biblical and historical support for its approach to the doctrine of salvation. Some theologians recognize the need for an account of salvation that includes each of these, though they may place greater emphasis on one or the other. Sometimes this greater emphasis is founded on a judgment about where the weight of Scripture is placed; sometimes it is founded on a "pastoral" judgment about which emphasis is most needed in the church at the time. Each of these views is also intertwined with views about the work of Christ, the nature of sin, and the character of the Christian life. As you read about the doctrine of salvation, consider how these relationships are worked out in a particular theologian's work.

The Meaning of Salvation

The Bible uses many images and concepts to give more specific content to the term "salvation" — forgiveness, justification, sanctification, righteousness, perfection, liberation, reconciliation, peace, and more. For this reason, it is difficult to focus on a smaller list of terms that is fully representative of different treatments of the doctrine of salvation. Often, the most important term for salvation in a particular theology is intertwined with other aspects of the doctrine of salvation. So, for example, a theology that treats salvation as primarily individual in scope will also tend toward certain meanings for salvation.

Even if the meaning of salvation is conceived broadly, its development will be influenced by the scope of salvation. For example, if a particular theology presents salvation as primarily individual, then any "liberation" theme will be focused on the individual, not on the corporate or cosmic dimension. In this case, salvation may mean the liberation of the individual from guilt and shame. In a more cosmic-centered doctrine of salvation, liberation will be the freeing of all creation from the burden of sin.

If we consider the earlier list of biblical terms for salvation, we see that some terms lend themselves to a particular view of the scope of salvation. And if we think a little more broadly, we also recognize that the scope and meaning of salvation are also intertwined with the doctrine of sin and the doctrine of the atonement. For example, the salvation of individuals and salvation as forgiveness fit more easily with sin as personal disobedience and Christ's atonement as a payment for the penalty of my sin. In another theology, a corporate view of salvation may fit easily with salvation as reconciliation. And these two may fit well with a particular view of atonement as the making of peace and sin as alienation.

Most theologies are not as narrowly focused or as simple as my description here. Most will consider several of the biblical terms for salvation, though each will generally place a primary emphasis on one or another of them. As you read, look for the interconnections among the doctrines of salvation, sin, and atonement. These interconnections will help you understand the perspective, and the strengths and weaknesses, of a particular theology.

It is also the case that particular theological traditions have particular emphases on salvation. As I noted at the beginning of this chapter, this is one of the doctrines that often divides theological traditions and various "churches." The most famous division occurred in the sixteenth century, when two groups argued over the meaning of "justification." These two groups split apart — we know them today as Catholics and Protestants. But to make things more complicated, some Catholics and Protestants have met together many times over the last decade and have agreed that the arguments that divided them in the sixteenth century are no longer reasons for distrusting each other. These groups have not reunited in a formal and organizational way, but they are beginning to cooperate with one another in various ways. Some now have rules and agreements that allow them to participate in the Eucharist together. (The Eucharist is discussed in chapter 9.) Others are working together on social and political issues.

In spite of this kind of coming together, however, you will generally find that each theological tradition has developed a particular emphasis for the meaning of salvation. Though there are always exceptions, Lutherans tend to emphasize justification, Baptists emphasize forgiveness, and liberation theologians emphasize liberation. However, these are not rigid categories that clearly separate theological traditions. Catholics talk about forgiveness as much as Baptists do, though they talk about it differently. Lutherans don't talk only about justification, they also talk about sanctification. And Presbyterians also talk about both. Similarly, liberation theologians, as I discuss in other chapters, come from a variety of traditions — they may be Catholic, Baptist, Methodist, or any other tradition. And Pentecostals talk about liberation, though they usually give it a meaning different from that of liberation theologians.

One other understanding of salvation should be identified: the notion of salvation as "deification." To most Western Christians this idea sounds heretical — it sounds like the teaching of some fringe group. But in fact, it has a long and honored tradition in the Eastern Orthodox tradition of Christianity. This tradition has developed separate (for the most part) from the Western tradition of Catholic and Protestant Christianity, but it may make a legitimate (though disputed) claim to be the oldest form of Christianity. In this tradition they teach a doctrine of salvation that argues that in Jesus Christ God descended to us so that we could be raised up to God. They do not mean that we become "gods," but they do teach that we become "godlike" by our identification with Jesus Christ. What this godlikeness means is very carefully developed in Eastern Orthodoxy. Although the notion of deification sounds strange to most Western ears, its development can bring a new and rich addition to our doctrine of salvation.

The Order of Salvation

This aspect of the doctrine of salvation (in Latin, *ordo salutis*) is concerned with the order of the events in salvation. This topic was energetically discussed during the Reformation of the sixteenth century and for some time afterward. Today, some theologians believe that the topic leads us away from important issues in the doctrine of salvation, but others continue to argue its relevance and incorporate it into their theologies.

Theologies that make the order of salvation an important part of their doctrine tend to identify with or be strongly influenced by one of the traditions of the Reformation period: Lutheran, Reformed (that is, Calvinist), or Catholic. Lutheran theologians regard the death of Christ as the first "act" in the order of salvation. This act is external to us, but makes it possible for us to receive the effects of Christ's death through faith. The Reformed tradition believes salvation has an entirely different set of events, not just a different order. In this tradition, rooted in a concentration on God's predestination, salvation begins with God's determination to save some human beings and progresses to the death of Christ for the salvation of those God has determined to save, then to the effective calling of the chosen, the regeneration of those called, and consequently to their coming to faith and persevering in faith to the end of life. Finally, for Catholics salvation begins (for those not baptized as infants — discussed in chapter 9) when we are convicted by God's justice so that we then repent of our sins. Salvation continues as we are baptized and by that baptism receive the benefits of Christ's death.

Each of these traditions also has internal tensions and disagreements concerning details of the order of salvation, but within the Reformed tradition one disagreement particularly stands out: that between Calvinism and Arminianism. This debate is complex and long-standing. My purpose here is not to explain it fully, but merely to make you aware of its dimensions. The disagreement is generated by the work of two theologians, John Calvin (1509-64) and James (or "Jacobus") Arminius (1560-1609). Calvin was a first-generation leader of the Protestant Reformation whose teaching on salvation emphasized God's sovereignty in predestining whom God would save and then irresistibly accomplishing that salvation. For Calvin, following the teaching of Augustine (354-430) and Luther, all the energy and work that accomplishes salvation comes from God. Arminius, an early student of Calvin's theology, raised several questions about Calvin's doctrine of salvation after Calvin's death. These questions and Arminius's other writings presented an order of salvation that begins not with God's predestining whom God will save, but with God foreknowing who will believe. The differences between Calvin and Arminius are subtle but important. In essence, Arminius places more weight on the human ability to participate in salvation. For him God's work in salvation is resistible, requiring human response. Though salvation is only by God's grace, humans are enabled by God's grace to respond and to participate.

These differences produced a lot of controversy and eventually led to a meeting of Calvin's and Arminius's theological descendants at the Synod of Dordt (1619). This synod sided with the traditional interpretation of Calvin's doctrine of salvation. Since that time, Calvinists and Arminians have often clashed, sometimes bitterly. Calvin's theology has traditionally been dominant among the "Reformed" churches (Dutch Reformed, Christian Reformed, Reformed Church in America), Presbyterians, the Puritans, some Baptists, and a variety of others. Arminius's theology has traditionally been dominant among Methodists (in a form not directly derived from Arminius), some Baptists, and Pentecostals. Because the influence of this controversy is so wide, most theologies consider in some form the issues it raises.

The Means of Salvation

How are people saved? If you are familiar with a particular Christian tradition, this probably sounds like a strange question. People "get saved" or become Christians in a particular way that is familiar and typical. But this process or event looks different in different churches.

The greatest differences in the means of salvation lie between the Protestant and Catholic traditions. These differences have often been divisive and have led to suspicion, misunderstanding, and condemnation. Even as I write this, it is difficult to convey the differences without misrepresenting one tradition to those who are familiar with the other. That is, to Protestants the Catholic understanding of the means of salvation seems strange, and to Catholics the Protestant understanding seems strange. In Protestant churches salvation is by "faith alone." (This phrase is one of the defining mottoes of the Protestant Reformation.) One becomes a Christian by believing what one hears in the preaching of the gospel. In the Catholic Church salvation is also by faith, but that faith is expressed through partaking of "the sacraments." (The concept of sacrament will be explained more fully in chapter 10.) Traditionally, Catholics have identified seven sacraments, the most prominent being baptism and Eucharist (called "the Lord's Supper" or "communion" in many other churches). Here's a simple way of putting it that risks misunderstanding and oversimplification: in Protestant churches baptism and Eucharist are things you do if you are a Christian; in Catholic churches baptism and Eucharist are what you do to be a Christian.

Good Quote

Conclusion

The differences we have considered in this chapter are differences in detail. We should not allow them to obscure the central and significant agreement that marks the great tradition of Christian theology — that salvation is found in Jesus Christ. Whatever the scope, meaning, order, and means of salvation, Christian theology converges on this point: Jesus Christ is Savior. In most theologies, even the details are more a matter of emphasis and less a matter of excluding another position. The differences in details that we encounter in our study of theology may usually be woven together into a tapestry that presents the beauty of salvation in Jesus Christ — in all its glory through many colors and tones.

CHAPTER 10

Church

Like salvation, the doctrine of the church is one of the Christian doctrines where our differences are usually obvious and sometimes divisive. All sorts of Christians — Baptists, Catholics, Methodists, Pentecostals, Presbyterians — may generally agree on most doctrines and deeply disagree on ecclesiology — the doctrine of the church. Here we have to be careful not to be confused by the terms. In this chapter the "doctrine of the church" means "what is taught *about* the church." In other places it may refer to "what the church teaches about God, Christ, humankind, and so on." Thus, to avoid possible confusion I am going to use the less familiar word "ecclesiology" for doctrine of the church. One more distinction is needed: that between "ecclesiological" and "ecclesiastical." "Ecclesiastical" is usually a synonym for "church." So when theologians write "ecclesiastical tradition," they simply mean "church tradition." "Ecclesiological" refers to the thinking that undergirds, shapes, guides, and describes the church: it is "thinking about the church." Both terms — "ecclesiastical" and "ecclesiological" — come from the Greek word in the NT that we translate "church": *ekklesia.*

Many Christians learn the doctrine of the church simply by growing up in or becoming members of a particular church. Churches often don't spend a lot of time explicitly teaching ecclesiology; they expect members to learn it through the im-

106

plicit ways it is taught in the actual life of the church. When we think more formally about ecclesiology, several issues may come up: the marks of the church, the mission of the church, the structure of the church, and the "activities" of the church, among others.

Some of these issues are more important in certain churches than in others. If you have been formed by one particular church, you may find the ecclesiological concerns of other churches to be strange. As you think more formally about the ecclesiology of your own church, you may also discover surprising, even disturbing, things about your own ecclesiological tradition. At times this process may be a bit scary, but I hope that in the end it will strengthen you as a follower of Jesus Christ.

One of the complex issues that runs throughout ecclesiology is how we think about the church. Do we think of the church primarily as one institution among many in our society? If so, then our thinking about the church may be dominated by sociological categories. Do we think of the church primarily as a means to my attaining certain goals? Then we are going to think of the church instrumentally, that is, as an instrument to be used to achieve certain ends. In the context of Christian doctrine, these and other ways of thinking about the church should be subordinate to thinking theologically about the church. This means that our ecclesiology must be rooted in the Bible and in other Christian doctrines. In this case, our ecclesiology will be explicitly shaped by our convictions about God, Christ, the Holy Spirit, atonement and salvation, and humankind.

Marks of the Church

Different churches mean different things when they speak about the "marks" of the church. Some churches use the language of "marks" as a way of distinguishing between "true" or "faithful" churches and "false" or "unfaithful" churches. Some traditions have a well-established and clear list of marks. Others may seldom speak about them. This doesn't mean they have no such concept; it usually means they have other language for the same or similar concepts.

In many traditions the marks of the church are identified by the language of the Apostles' Creed or the Nicene Creed. The longer of the two creeds confesses the church as "one, holy, catholic, and apostolic." In those churches where the creed is regularly confessed, these words identify the marks of the church.

As you may imagine, these traditions and the theologians within them direct considerable energy into a clear and persuasive account of the meaning of these words. For those Christians who are unfamiliar with the creed and its ecclesiology, these words at first seem strange and perhaps wrong. At the same time, we must remember that the ecclesiology represented by these creeds has shaped the church for centuries. Even those who come from "noncreedal" traditions have found lots of guidance from these words.

"One, holy, catholic, and apostolic" is explained in different ways by theologians. But one word in that list often requires special explanation: "catholic." Today, we have come to use that word in a narrow way to refer only to the church that is in direct relationship to the bishop of Rome — that is, the pope. In other words, when we hear "catholic," we think Roman Catholic. But "catholic" has another meaning, more like "universal." So when Christians confess "one, holy, *catholic*, apostolic church," we are confessing the belief in a church that transcends all human boundaries, whether race, nation, sex, class, education, or any other boundary we may create. In this sense the "catholic" church is not limited to one nation, one race, one language, one . . . anything.

Of course, the other marks of the church may get special attention as well, and may be developed in different ways. Each may seem to be a difficult, unusual mark for a church that doesn't seem to be one or holy or apostolic. Yet, the church through the centuries has confessed this, and many theologians give credible, biblical accounts of these marks as characteristic of the church.

Other traditions may supplement the creedal marks of the church or may set them aside. At the time of the Protestant Reformation in the sixteenth century, the creedal marks were used to deny that the protesters were part of the church. After all, there is only one church, so it was claimed, and that one church says the protesters and reformers (people like Martin Luther, Huldrych Zwingli, and John Calvin) are wrong. In this conflict, people like Luther argued that while the true church is "one, holy, catholic, and apostolic," these words do not tell us which "church" is the true church. So the Reformers wrestled with this issue and concluded that the true church is one where the word of God is faithfully proclaimed and the sacraments (they meant especially baptism and communion) rightly celebrated. Then, of course, they argued that these things were marks of their church but not of other churches.

(Here I need to warn you about a problem with words. The phrase "Roman Catholic Church" is not one that the Reformers used. At the time of the Reformation, the names for churches we use today — Lutheran, Presbyterian, Roman Catholic, Baptist, Methodist — were not in use. So we may be clear but chronologically wrong when we apply today's terms to those earlier controversies.)

Finally, still other traditions hold other understandings of the marks of the church. Anabaptist churches, and some others, argue that suffering is a mark of the true church, as is church discipline, or more plainly, discipleship.

The Mission of the Church

What is the purpose of the church? Is there only one purpose? And if there is, are there various ways of fulfilling that purpose? Are there perhaps different facets to some one purpose? Or perhaps the mission of the church varies from time to time and place to place.

As theologians formulate the mission of the church, their accounts may vary widely. Some theologians develop the doctrine of the church in light of a theological claim, such as "the mission of the church is to bring glory to God." It is important to root our ecclesiology in such a claim, but we must also specify what the church is called to do in order to glorify God.

Of course, the primary means of bringing glory to God is by our worship. In some theologies the worship of God plays a significant role and receives considerable attention as a source for theology. In other theologies it may be treated briefly or left out altogether as a topic.

Most theologies direct some attention to "witness" as a description of the mission of the church. This witness may be specified as "proclaiming the gospel," where proclaiming is understood as verbal preaching. Another ecclesiology may also declare that the church is to proclaim the gospel, but with the sense of "proclaiming in deed," that is, in action rather than words. Another ecclesiology may declare that the church is called to "word and deed." Others may call the church to caring for the poor and oppressed, and still others may call the church beyond caring for the poor and oppressed to "liberation of the poor and oppressed." And in the midst of this, many ecclesiologies will wrestle with the form of the church's obligation to bear witness.

What you should recognize here is the interconnection between any account of the mission of the church and other theological convictions. A theologian's account of the doctrine of salvation will be intertwined with his or her account of the mission of the church. Is salvation only or primarily about "saving" individuals? Then the mission of the church will be shaped accordingly, and little if any emphasis will be placed on changing the structures of society. Is salvation only or primarily about changing the structures of society that oppress people? Then the mission of the church will be focused on social change. Other accounts of salvation will yield still different accounts of the mission of the church. And any account of the mission of the church will be deeply intertwined with convictions about the relationship between the church and the world.

Finally, any account of the mission of the church will be working out the complex relationship between biblical teaching and current context. That is, an ecclesiology may have a well-worked-out account of the mission of the church, but that account may not always tell the church what is needed in a particular situation. For example, some ecclesiologies may teach that the primary mission of the church is to "make disciples." That teaching may be deeply rooted in a firm conviction about the teaching of Matthew 28:18-20. But that teaching doesn't tell the church how to carry out that mission in its particular cultural context. What does it mean to "make disciples" in a culture where Christianity has been the dominant religion for two hundred years? What does "make disciples" mean in a culture where there is deep poverty, disease, and suffering? These kinds of challenges make the work of theology a joyous, never ending task made possible only by God's grace and wisdom.

The Structure of the Church

By structure of the church, I am referring to the way ecclesiologies understand the organization of the church, in short, what may be called church government. Sometimes the possibilities for structuring the church are neatly divided into congregational, presbyterian, and episcopal categories. These terms refer to historic differences among churches, but the lines are not always so clear today.

We may achieve some ecclesiological clarity by asking who has the authority to call and dismiss the pastor or priest, who owns the church property, and who decides controversies over doctrine and practice. In a congregational church government, the entire membership of a local congregation has ultimate authority. But sometimes congregational ecclesiology also allows for the election of elders or deacons, a smaller group that decides many of the issues in the church. And some congregational traditions divide responsibilities between elders and deacons.

In presbyterian church government, final authority for most decisions resides in the presbytery, which is made up of people who have been ordained to ministry and live in a certain geographical area. But even the presbytery leaves many decisions to the local congregation and their ruling board, especially in North America. Nevertheless, the presbytery has final say on most matters. Thus, if a congregation becomes unhappy with the denomination and wants to leave, their church property is owned not by them but by the presbytery, and the financial settlements often take years to be resolved, often in the courts. On other matters, a presbyterian ecclesiology usually has other levels of authority made up of representatives from local presbyteries. These governing bodies decide matters that cannot be resolved in local presbyteries or matters of doctrine and practice that concern more than just a local presbytery.

In episcopal ecclesiology the church, including the ordained clergy, is governed by bishops. The bishops of the church are the episcopacy. Bishops preside primarily over a geographical territory, a diocese, though they may send out missionaries or educators from their dioceses to some other part of the world and still maintain authority over them. In North America the situation can be confusing because we have here a church called the Episcopal Church, U.S.A (ECUSA). However, this church is not the only church in North America that has an episcopal ecclesiology. And ECUSA is a part of the worldwide Anglican Church, or Church of England, that is in relationship with the archbishop of Canterbury. Thus, in other parts of the world we have, for example, the Anglican Church in Canada. (You can guess that the war fought at the end of the eighteenth century might have something to do with the fact that we do not have an "Anglican Church in the U.S.A.")

The Episcopal Church is not the only episcopal ecclesiology, though it is the most obvious example because of its name. Another example, perhaps more purely episcopal, is the Roman Catholic Church. Of course, if you know that the Church of England (Anglican Church) broke away from the Roman Catholic

Church, you might also guess that they would be similar. Likewise, the Methodist church, which developed from the Anglican Church, also has bishops, though they function in different ways. In all of these examples, bishops often consult with congregations and with other priests or pastors before making significant decisions. Still, the final authority rests in bishops.

We may observe, then, that although the lines between versions of church government are not always absolute, in the end there are significant differences. One difference at the beginning of the twenty-first century has to do with the question of who may be ordained. In the Catholic Church, of course, priests are normally unmarried men. In other churches there is continuing controversy over whether women should be ordained. In still others there is controversy over whether homosexuals (men or women) should be ordained. In some churches the questions have been decided, though they may continue to provoke controversy. In other churches the questions are still very much open and unsettled.

In most ecclesiologies there is some recognition that settling the form of church government is not central to the gospel. In many ecclesiologies, you may even find an acknowledgment that the biblical teaching on this matter is unclear. Thus, for some theologians church government is a matter of historical and cultural accident. These theologians usually charge us with being as faithful to the gospel as we can be in the particular form of church government that we find ourselves working with. But for other theologians church government is not a matter of indifference. For them the form is crucial to being faithful to the gospel. And for some ecclesiologies, those "churches" not in relationship to their "one true church" are in fact not true churches, though some of their members may still be saved by God's grace.

"Activities" of the Church

"Activities" is an awkward, horrible word for this section of the chapter. But the fact that I could not find another word is an indication of the difficulty I face in writing on this topic. In this section I will introduce you to what some churches call "ordinances" and others call "sacraments." The two ordinances or sacraments that almost all churches agree on are baptism and communion (or Lord's Supper or Eucharist). A few traditions add foot washing as a third ordinance or sacrament, and other traditions recognize seven sacraments. The situation is made a bit more complex by some Christian traditions (such as the Salvation Army and the Society of Friends, or "Quakers") that argue that baptism and communion are "spiritual" activities that do not require the actual use of water, bread, and wine.

Because baptism and communion are physical activities, we may be tempted to focus on how these are done — how much water is used for baptism, who is eligible for it, how often communion is celebrated, how it is organized, and who may participate. These details are important and reveal a lot about an ecclesiological tradition. In a full-scale theology they may receive a lot of attention as a way of developing an ecclesiology. Here I will introduce you to some basic concerns that will help you approach these other questions with some understanding.

In some churches these activities are named ordinances because they are commanded, or "ordered," by Jesus Christ. In other traditions they are called sacraments because they "mediate" or transport God's grace to us. These differences in terminology have deep historical roots and represent significantly different ways of looking at the world. For people who have been formed by one of these traditions, the other tradition can look very strange. Of course, all traditions recognize Jesus' command to do these things (Matt. 28:18-20; 1 Cor. 11:23-26), and all traditions recognize the working of God's grace. But they describe these realities in different ways and give them different emphases in their traditions and in their ecclesiologies.

For some, these activities are the heart of the church and, therefore, the heart of the good news of Jesus Christ. For them, my use of "activities" as a description is unfamiliar and inappropriate at best. For others, these activities come very close to being accessories: they are good things to do, but little if anything important would be lost if we ceased to do them.

One of the central tasks of any ecclesiology is to describe clearly how the command to practice these ordinances or sacraments both reflects what God has done in Jesus Christ and draws us more deeply into the continuing work of Christ through the Holy Spirit. This may be accomplished in different ways depending upon the ecclesiastical tradition to which the ecclesiology is responsible. One of the encouraging developments over the last several decades is the way that many churches have come together and found ways to acknowledge the unity in the midst of the different ways that we talk about and practice baptism and communion.

Conclusion

The life of the church is lived before a watching world. In its life the church often appears to be divided. But if we think carefully about the church and develop an ecclesiology that describes our common theology, then we can begin to see the unity that we have in the gospel even as that gospel is lived out in a variety of ways, all of which contribute to the life of the church which is the one body of Christ.

CHAPTER 11

Last Things

Isn't it appropriate that this last chapter is concerned with "the last things"? And yet, the phrase "last things" can be misleading since it implies that we haven't thought about these things until now. In fact, however, we have been thinking about these last things from the beginning. In another way, these are the last things because although they have been "in the picture" from the beginning, we are only now bringing them into the center and focusing on them.

The special theological term for the study of the last things is "eschatology," which comes from the Greek word *eschatos,* "last." Most theologians discuss four last things under the study of eschatology. They may vary a little bit, but usually they are: (1) the return of Christ, (2) the general resurrection, (3) the last judgment, and (4) the final state. Most of this chapter will be concerned with these four topics, variations on them, and more detail about them.

But first I must tell you about a larger eschatological approach in theology. Just above, I noted that in a sense eschatology has been with us from the beginning of our study, not just here at the end. This eschatological emphasis or perspective is an important part of a lot of twentieth-century theology.

To understand what an eschatological perspective on theology means, think about two different ways to watch a movie about a murder mystery. The first time you see the movie in the theater, you don't know how it ends (unless a friend who has already seen the movie gives it away). Who committed the murder? Will the murderer get away? Who will still be alive at the end? Now, imagine that several months later the movie is being broadcast on television. This time when you watch the movie, you know the ending, so you watch it very differently. If it is really well made, you may pick up clues and notice nuances that you missed the first time you saw it.

An eschatological approach to theology is like seeing the movie the second time. When we begin studying God, we already know something about what God has done in Jesus Christ. And when we begin studying Jesus Christ, we know that he was crucified and has been raised from the dead. So, we have a very different perspective from Moses and the Israelites and from the first disciples when they began to follow Jesus. We have an *eschatological* perspective.

This eschatological perspective does not mean that we know everything. It just means that we have an angle and some further knowledge from which to view things. This eschatological perspective on theology differs in another important way from my movie analogy. The movie comes to an end; history has not. So eschatology not only gives us a perspective looking back, it also gives us a perspective looking forward.

Several theologians have made important contributions to an eschatological perspective in theology. (Wolfhart Pannenberg and Jürgen Moltmann are two of the most influential.) These theologians differ in the ways they develop this perspective, sometimes subtly, sometimes obviously. All of them emphasize the importance of history and of God's work in history viewed eschatologically, that is, viewed from the end of history that has already been revealed in Jesus Christ.

For most of them the resurrection of Jesus is the end (or goal) of history already revealed. They may differ in their explanation of the resurrection (see chapter 4), but it is this event, which has already happened, that reveals to us where history is headed. As the revelation of the goal, the resurrection of Jesus also tells us how to interpret the rest of history. But even as I use this language of end and goal, these theologians would also remind us that the goal or end of history is not the end of the story. It is really just the conclusion of this chapter or episode, or in the language of Scripture, the end of this age and the beginning of a new creation.

Before we look more closely at the four last things, I must make one more introductory point. In different parts of the church around the world, eschatology has been given different amounts of attention and different aspects have been emphasized. In North America and especially in the United States, more attention has been given to the details and dating of the return of Christ than in other parts of the world. This emphasis and the specific way it is developed in popular teaching and literature, like the series of novels called *Left Behind,* have left many inside and outside the church with the impression that there is only one way that Christian theology approaches the return of Christ. That is not true. As you study Christian doctrine, you will discover other approaches to eschatology that may also claim support in the teaching of Scripture and the church.

The Return of Jesus Christ

The NT is filled with the declaration by Jesus and by his disciples that, after his death and resurrection, he will "go away" for a while and then return. The promise of his return is tied to the completion, or consummation, of his work. Thus, how this return is envisioned in any particular theology is also tied to the perception of what the work of Christ is. The relationship between these two doctrines — salvation and consummation — is usually complex, though salvation is usually the dominant doctrine. In other words, what a theology teaches about salvation strongly shapes what it teaches about the return of Christ.

The return of Christ is often tied to language about the millennium, the thousand years referred to in Revelation 20. How this passage affects eschatological thinking about the return of Christ depends in part on how one understands the language of the book of Revelation. Is the language literal or symbolic? That is, does the thousand years of Revelation 20 refer to a literal thousand years that can be counted down in history? Or is "a thousand years" a symbol of a very long time? Or does it symbolize some reality other than the passage of years? In our age of precise measurements and careful dating of events, we have a strong tendency to read the biblical passages in literal terms. This is natural for us, but many who study the world of the Bible remind us that it would not have been so natural for the authors of Scripture.

So, in many theologies the return of Christ is correlated in some fashion with the millennium. If the view is that Christ will return prior to the millennium in order to bring it about, then the position taken is called premillennialism. If the view is that Christ will return after the millennium to bring this age to an end, then the position is called postmillennialism. If the view is that the language of Scripture refers to a reality that cannot be dated by the passage of a set number of years, then the position is called amillennialism. This last view holds that Christ will return to consummate his work, but not that the "thousand years" of Revelation 20 refers to the passage of a set number of years.

In North American Christianity, particularly its more conservative traditions, these millennial views have in the past been sources of division among Christians. For some, that is still the case. But for many others the return of Christ and the completion of his work in a new creation are more important than a specific position on the timing of his return. As a result of this conviction, many refuse to enter into the old controversies and instead are seeking new ways to talk about the promise of Christ's return.

The General Resurrection

The "general resurrection" is an awkward way of reminding us that one of the results of Christ's return is the bodily resurrection of the dead. Throughout most of its history, the church has confessed belief in the bodily resurrection of human beings who have died, on the basis of Christ's own bodily resurrection as described in passages like Luke 24. In recent years, however, under the pressure of skepticism about resurrection and the over-spiritualizing of Christianity, the resurrection has sometimes come to stand for the continuing existence of disembodied spirits after their bodies have disintegrated. In other words, some Christians and some theologies have abandoned belief in the bodily resurrection. In its place, they confess that if there is any continuing personal existence after physical death, that continuing existence is purely spiritual.

This claim may sound right to many Christians, and seems quite "spiritual." But it abandons one of the central teachings of the Bible: that the God who sustains our lives for eternity is the same God who created life in its physical, that is, material, expression. Creation, including our bodies, is created by God to be good. And if this Creator God is also the Redeemer God, then the return of Christ to complete the work of redemption must include our bodies.

For those theologians who affirm this central teaching of the Bible and the church, at least two intriguing questions arise. First, how does God "resurrect" our bodies after they have indeed disintegrated after death and passed into the history of the universe, even, if I may be just a bit crude, after our bodies have become part of the food chain? Second, what happens to us between the time of our deaths and our resurrection at the return of Christ? These are the kinds of questions that can be delightful to think about. They are puzzles that can lead us into other insights and into the celebration of some of the mysteries of God's work that remind us that we will never fully comprehend God and God's work. If we did, then of course we would have a human-sized God — who wouldn't be much of a god then. The answers to these questions are not at all clear in Scripture or the tradition, but we can delight God, and delight in God, by considering the possibilities with an appropriate humility.

The Last Judgment

In our present cultural climate, the last judgment can be a very difficult topic to think about, because it seems to run directly in the face of the importance we place on tolerance and not judging others. In the light of Christian history, the idea of judgment can also call up sinful moments in the church when we have been very willing to pronounce judgment and execute that judgment on others.

But the last judgment of God is part of the teaching of Scripture and the church, so we cannot simply set it aside. In developing an account of the last judgment, theologians draw out different emphases. Some focus on the status of individuals, the question of who is saved and who is not, who is forgiven their sins and received into God's new creation and who is not forgiven and excluded from the new creation. In this instance, a theologian must also give an account of the basis for the judgment that is made. In some parts of Christianity, this question has led to lively debates about the importance of coming to faith in Christ in this life, and following from that, the status of those who never hear the gospel of Jesus Christ in this life and thus never have an opportunity to believe. This also becomes a place where attention may be directed to the status of followers of other religions and of no religion.

Other theologians place little emphasis on the question of individual judgment. Instead, they emphasize that the last judgment describes God's discernment of all that is good and redeemable and thus has a place in the new creation. Here the status of individuals may receive little attention; often this approach is accompanied by the belief that all human beings will be redeemed by God's grace in Christ. The last judgment does not determine who will be redeemed; it entails God judging between what of people's lives can be redeemed and brought into the new creation and what of their lives cannot be redeemed but must instead be excluded. God's discriminating judgment goes beyond individual lives to also consider the work of humankind — our culture.

In both of these approaches to the last judgment, the best theologies do not isolate their accounts from God's character or God's ultimate intention to bring the work of Christ to completion and set the world right. To accomplish this, God, who is holy, loving, just, righteous, gracious, merciful, and so much more, must, in the end, judge the world.

The Final State

In the last things, the "final state" identifies the culmination of God's work in this age and the beginning of the new. The best way to talk about the final state is to use the language of "new creation" or "new heavens and a new earth," from Revelation 21.

Often, however, Christians will talk of this final state as "heaven and hell." But what those terms mean to people often turns out to be misleading. When Christians talk about heaven, they usually think of a place that is alien to us, strange and wispy, where we float around as disembodied spirits free from the burdens of creation. But this way of thinking perpetuates one of the problems that I have been identifying throughout this book: the common mistake today of denying the ultimate goodness of creation and God's work to redeem creation from its captivity to sin.

So the better way to think about and talk about the final state is "new creation." Theologians will differ in their accounts of this new creation: How much can we actually know about it now? How much can we speculate? How much continuity is there between this creation and the new? These questions again seem to fall mostly in the realm of uncertain reflection on the future. But reverent speculation helps us give substance today to a future that we know in little detail, except for the confidence that as the work of the triune God who is holy and loving, the new creation will be glorious beyond our imagination, beyond what we could even bear to know in our present state. The privilege of the work of theology is to begin even now to catch a glimpse of God's eternal glory as it has been revealed to us in Jesus Christ.

Timeline

	100	
St. Irenaeus (~120-203)		
Arius (~260-336)		
Constantine (~285-337)		
St. Athanasius (~296-373)	325	Council of Nicea
Apollinaris (~310-390)		
Cappadocians		
St. Basil (329-379)		
St. Gregory of Nazianzus (~329-390)	381	Council of Constantinople (I)
St. Gregory of Nyssa (~334-395)		
St. Augustine (354-430)		
	431	Council of Ephesus (I)
	451	Council of Chalcedon
Nestorius (386-451)		
Monophysites		
Monothelites		
	~589	"Filioque" clause introduced
St. John of Damascus (~675-749)		
	1054	Great Schism (East and West)
St. Anselm (1033-1109)		
St. Abelard (1079-1142)		
St. Thomas Aquinas (1225-1274)		